Mexico City

WORLD FOOD

Mexico City

Heritage Recipes for Classic Home Cooking

JAMES OSELAND

with Jenna Leigh Evans
Photographs by James Roper

TEN SPEED PRESS
California | New York

This photo: Miners' Enchiladas (page 70). Page ii: Mexican-Style Stewed Zucchini and Poblanos (page 90). Page iv: grilled corn. Page v: mariachis aboard a boat in the main canal of Xochimilco.

Contents

Ciudad
Satélite

San Martín
Xochinahuac

Lindavista

San Bartolo
Atepehuacan

Boulevares

AZCAPOTZALCO

GUSTAVO A
MADERO

San Pedro
Xalpa

San Juan
de Aragón

Vallejo

Naucalpan
de Juárez

Tlatelolco

Tepito

MIGUEL
HIDALGO

Paseo de la Reforma

CATEDRAL

BENITO JUÁREZ
INTERNATIONAL
AIRPORT

Polanco

Centro
Histórico

VENUSTIANO
CARRANZA

Lomas de
Chapultepec

Colonia
Juárez

MERCADO DE
SAN JUAN

Chapultepec
Park

La Condesa

CUAUHTEMOC

MERCADO
DE LA MERCED

La Roma

Jardín
Balbuena

Escandón

Algarín

IZTACALCO

Bosques de
las Lomas

Nápoles

San Pedro
de los Pinos

MEXICO CITY

Del Valle

Santa Fé

BENITO
JUÁREZ

MERCADO
PORTALES

CENTRAL DE
ABASTOS

Mixcoac

ÁLVARO
OBREGÓN

MERCADO
LA NUEVA VIGA

Guadalupe
del Moral

San Mateo
Tlaltenango

San Ángel

Coyoacán

Pueblo
Culhuacán

San Juan
Xalpa

Olivar de los
Padres

COYOACÁN

Jardines de
Pedregal

Ajusco

MAGDALENA
CONTRERAS

Toriello
Guerra

Acoxpa

Héroes de
Padierna

San Andrés
Totoltepec

XOCHILMILCO

TLALPAN

SCALE

0 1 2 3 4 5 kilometres

0 1 2 3 4 5 miles

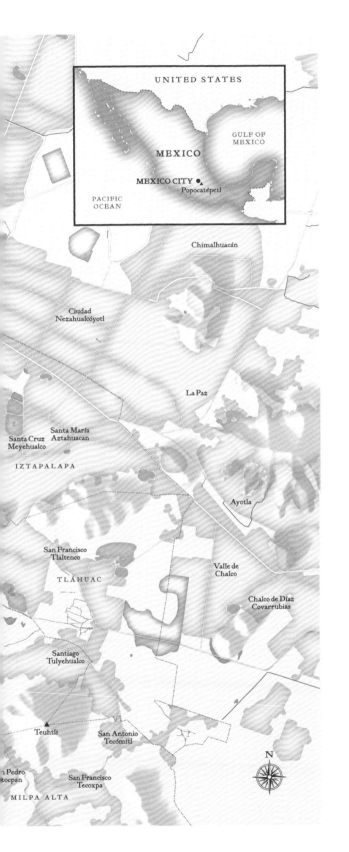

Lush Land

The Valle de Mexico, where Mexico City is situated, is a former lakebed seamed with volcanoes both dormant and active, including Popocatépetl, an often smoke-plumed mountain nearly 18,000 feet high. Since approximately AD 100, waves of successive cultures have enjoyed this land's fecundity: the Toltecs, Acolhua, Chichimeca, Tepaneca, and Aztecs. After the Spanish Conquest in 1519, the inter-mingling of the native population with the Europeans created a citizenry with mixed and complex ethnic roots. With roughly 22 million people in total, contemporary Mexico City is the political, economic, and social hub of Mexico; it is also the unofficial capital of Latin America. Its multiple and crowded municipalities and neighborhoods sprawl in all directions, making it the largest metropolitan area in the Western Hemisphere and the second largest in the world after Tokyo. Yet, even though the city has expanded to the point where it imperils its surrounding environment, because of the fertility of the soil (and the devotion of its people to upholding traditional foodways), extensive farmland still exists within city limits. Mexico City's architecturally significant historic center, known as the Centro Histórico, is its jewel in the crown: the six-square-mile neighborhood has been declared a World Heritage Site by UNESCO.

CITY POPULATION *8,918,653*
METROPOLITAN POPULATION *21,782,378*
ELEVATION *7,200 feet*
CLIMATE *Subtropical highland*
AVERAGE HIGHS AND LOWS *71°F and 45°F*
LANGUAGES *Spanish, plus 68 indigenous languages (notably Nuahatl, Maya, and Mixtec)*
NUMBER OF MAJOR MUSEUMS *150*
SOCCER TEAMS *Cruz Azul, Club America, Pumas*

Lingering over family-style meals is central to the Mexico City lifestyle. Here, a multigenerational family enjoys Pork Rib and Vegetable Stew with Ancho and Pasilla Chiles (page 136).

1

Food from Hearth and Heart

Introduction

*Colorful heirloom corn
that will be cooked, ground
into masa, and patted into
blue-corn tortillas. Page xi:
a customer enjoys a taco in
La Merced Market.*

Many Citizens, One Cuisine

Some residents of Mexico City have roots there that date back generations; others have come more recently from places as far-flung as tropical Chiapas or remote villages on the Isla Guadalupe, an island off the southwest coast. Whether from a region best known for cloud forests or for cattle ranching, each resident brings his or her specific attitude to cooking and eating, influenced by both family and regional history. These myriad traditions have melded in the vast, fast-paced city to create a distinct sensibility at the table. It is a cuisine that defies easy description, yet it is recognizable to those who live there. It might have something to do with the casual adaptation of foods and techniques that come from elsewhere. Only in Mexico City, for instance, does the tamale get put on a crusty roll for a meal on the go—*guajolota*, the city's most popular breakfast. And then there is *mole poblano*, a sauce made from an array of dried chiles with a flavor profile to match. It originated in Puebla, where it is the star dish. But in Mexico City, it has been incorporated into the everyday, not so much a celebratory food as a mainstay, usually slathered atop enchiladas. Notwithstanding the metropolitan flair the city brings to cooking, however, the heart of its dining experience is the family meal, cooked at home.

A few faces of Mexico City, clockwise from top left: a street musician; Super Astro, otherwise known as Juan Zesati, a professional wrestler; a waiter at Contramar; Mónica Casanova, a multidisciplinary artist; Alam Méndez Florián, the chef at Pasillo de Humo; a waitress at a restaurant that specializes in Mexican chicken stew.

Victoria Hernández, a grandmother still stylish in her mid-sixties, stirs the bubbling stew with a wooden spoon and glances out the kitchen window.

Back in the village in Veracruz state, where she was raised, the morning stillness was broken by the crowing of roosters and the clopping of horses' hooves. Here in the Mexico City neighborhood of Tepito, where she lives now, the cars are already honking, and the street teems with sellers hawking their wares. A pushcart vendor is righting a toppled stack of papayas. Under a clothesline heavy with the week's washing, a couple of young boxers are throwing practice punches, and children have gathered to watch. The youngest girl among them spies Hernández at the window and raises her arm in greeting. She's one of the seven people that call the three-room apartment home.

Hernández waves back at the girl, making her smile, then places a few pasilla chiles onto the hot comal, a circular grill. Since antiquity, chiles have been a fundamental component in Mexican cuisine. They are used not only as a condiment but also as a primary ingredient, and a recipe often contains more than one variety. Indeed, the meal that Hernández is making today calls for two types of dried chile: The pasilla, with its glossy, crinkled skin, contributes an earthy flavor and a mild heat to dishes. The ancho, known as a poblano when fresh, is sweeter and adds a vibrant red hue. Ground into a paste, they will fortify the *mole de olla,* a rich stew made of bone-in pork and chunks of corn on the cob, zucchini, carrots, chayote, and potatoes.

Tepito has been crowded with itinerant street markets for nearly seven hundred years. The neighborhood has had a reputation for being a rough and lawless place since the Aztec era, and in that regard, little has changed. But while Hernández has lived here for five decades, she's proud to bring the quietness and simplicity of her Veracruz upbringing to her cooking style. The chiles toasting on the comal pop and release their sharp, smoky fragrance into the air. In a blue enamel stockpot, the pork is getting tender. She places the toasted chiles into hot water to soften.

A pair of small dogs comes bursting through the door, with Flora Ayala, Hernández's neighbor and friend, close behind. Ayala, beautiful and poised in her twenties, has come for some of her companion's sage advice and perhaps a bit of gossip. But she knows Hernández, who has a cleaning job that starts at six every evening, still has a lot of work ahead of her, so she seats herself at the table and starts peeling vegetables for the *mole de olla.*

As Hernández grinds the softened chiles along with spices and fried garlic in a blender, then strains that mixture into the pork broth, the women chat. Daily life, family, politics, the conundrums of the day—this conversational

aspect of meal preparation is not an exercise in biding time; it's an integral part of the cooking process. Hernández's teenaged granddaughter comes in to announce that there's a new man on the block selling very convincing *fayuca*—fakes, knockoffs, usually made in China—of the shoes everyone's wearing this season. But, she adds proudly, she was not taken in by his ruse.

Hernández puts fresh green beans and chunks of *calabacitas*, Mexico's smaller, lime-green zucchini, into the pot. "Clever princess, did you remember to get tortillas?" Her granddaughter claps her hands over her mouth—oops. "I'll do it right now," she says, dashing for the door.

"Wait—get another avocado while you're out. And bring your sisters in for lunch at three," Hernández tells the girl. "Tell your grandfather, too, if you can wake him." This last is a joke. Her husband, a parking attendant, works tirelessly, despite being in his seventies. Her granddaughter dashes out, whistling for the dogs to follow.

In her wake, Hernández's teenaged grandson comes in. Yes, he answers Hernández before she can ask, he *has* started the weekend's homework—his mother can testify to that. Hernández pours for him an *agua fresca*, cool water infused with juice or flavorings, in this case with *flor de jamaica*, hibiscus blossoms. It's a subtly sweet, sour, and refreshing drink that he gratefully gulps down.

By now the aroma is irresistible. Ayala stirs the stew, tastes it. "This is so delicious. Why is your cooking always better than food at a restaurant?"

"Because nothing tastes as good as it does at home," Hernández replies without hesitation.

This sentiment is held in the hearts of the city's cooks. Prepare the dishes presented in this book and you will connect to the heart of the way these people prepare food. Mexico City is inarguably famous for its street food. The dishes people make in their home kitchens, though, hold the essence of the cuisine, and are as joyfully colorful and diverse a human accomplishment as the city itself.

When you try your hand at these recipes, be patient. Cooking Mexican food is a relaxed, gradual process—true slow food. Begin, if you wish, with a simple yet essential dish like *salsa roja*, to be eaten with quesadillas hot off the stove, or with *frijoles refritos*, refried beans with onions and garlic. As you become more familiar with the methods and ingredients, try cooking something a bit more complex, such as *lomo adobado*, pork tenderloin in a thick sauce spiked with chiles and beer. Or you might make a big pot of wholesome *mole de olla* for your own family and friends. Señora Victoria Hernández would be honored if you did.

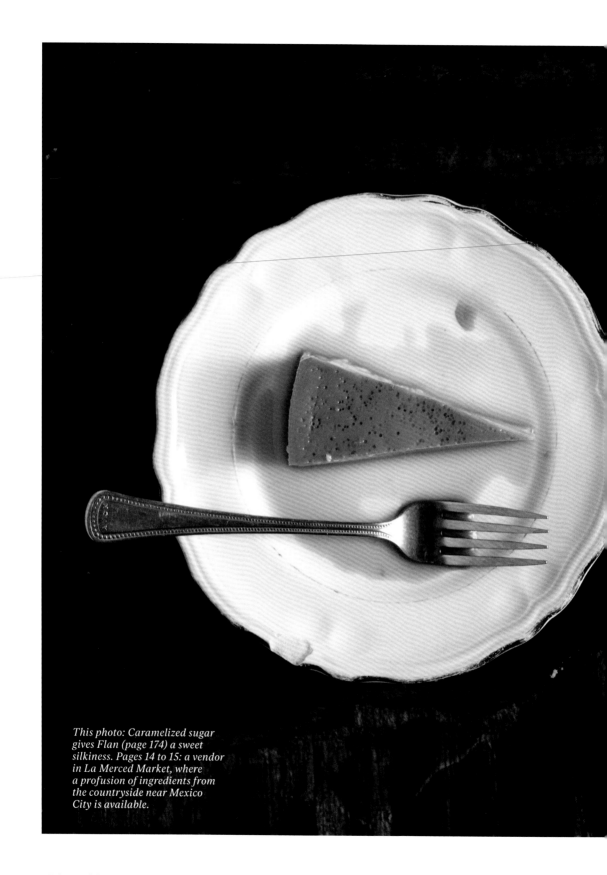

This photo: Caramelized sugar gives Flan (page 174) a sweet silkiness. Pages 14 to 15: a vendor in La Merced Market, where a profusion of ingredients from the countryside near Mexico City is available.

A cook circa 1910 uses traditional cookware to prepare a meal over a firewood stove.

*Above: Cheese Quesadillas (page 61).
Opposite: Crisp-Fried Taco Flutes
(page 61). Page 20: Pickled Chiles and
Vegetables with Thyme, Oregano,
and Bay Leaves (page 38), eaten as
a condiment with savory dishes.*

2

The Heat That Tames Hunger

Appetizers and Small Plates

Painter Alfredo Gavaldón holds a bowl containing the topping for Flank Steak and Avocado Tostadas (page 32).

Shrimp and árbol chiles transform pasta into a distinctly Mexican dish at Contramar, one of the city's most famous restaurants; recipe on page 34.

One way to understand how residents of Mexico City think of appetizers is to visit a *fonda*. This is a small establishment that, for a few pesos, serves a home-style meal, chiefly *comida* (what those outside of Mexico consider lunch), and usually according to a set menu of several courses.

One *fonda* in Centro Histórico happens to be located in the lobby of a bathhouse, and has a rococo swankiness that evidently crystallized around 1972, with gleaming marble floors, Naugahyde booths, and gilt mirrors, yet the dining space is not much larger than a living room. Here customers are waiting for the *patrona,* the "boss," who seats the newcomers, oversees the kitchen, tastes the food, and generally runs the show. Today's *patrona* is an imposing figure with immaculately coiffed hair who issues brisk instructions to the staff, but she is congenial with the clientele, seating them with a singsong, "Ah, good afternoon, what do you feel like for your soup course?" A *fonda* menu mirrors the traditional home meal, and that means starting with soup. Today's choice, the *patrona* says, is between *consomé de pollo* (chicken broth with vegetables) and *sopa de lentejas* (lentil soup).

Sopa de lentejas it is. She dispatches the order. Serene in spite of the pace, the cook cinches her yellow apron tighter and sets to work. Pots brimming with today's soups,

appetizers, first courses, and main dishes jostle for room on the stove top. As the cook lifts her ladle, steam mingles with air from outside.

Throughout the room, grateful diners are digging into the bowls that are being set before them. At the counter, a gentleman in a Stetson is rolling up a hot tortilla and dipping it into his *sopa de lentejas* with satisfaction. Those who have only eaten lentil soup north of the border might envision a comforting but unflashy dish—but this is Mexico City. Its base, seasoned with bacon and cilantro, has the usual earthy quality. Here and now, however, it is eaten with a big dollop of the *salsa verde* the cook is setting out on the tables. Made with charred tomatillos, garlic, and serrano chiles, the salsa brightens the soup's hearthside warmth with a garden freshness. The diners' enjoyment does not escape the cook, and she allows herself a smile of pride.

A small plate known as a *sopa seca* follows the soup course. This is usually either a rice or a pasta, which in this context the Mexican cook treats as a course unto itself, not just a side dish. One of the offerings at the *fonda* today is spaghetti that has been simmered in chipotle chiles and cream, then topped with rustic Cotija cheese. Another choice is *arroz borracho,* or "drunken rice." Simmered in beer and fragrant with garlic and onion, it gets its orange color from carrot and tomato and has a subtle depth of flavor. As satisfying as it is, there's just enough of it to whet the appetite

In Central de Abastos, the world's largest food market, a waitress deftly carries a tray on her head for easier transport.

for the main courses to come: Diners can choose from *chiles anchos rellenos*, battered and fried ancho chiles stuffed with cheese and served with tomato sauce, or *enchiladas mineras*, tortillas dipped in salsa and then fried, stuffed with chicken, and garnished with toppings.

Attend a party in Mexico City and you'll enter another realm, where appetizers and small plates reign supreme. There's nothing like a celebration for a chance to regale friends and family with an array of tempting offerings. A host doesn't need to craft a full meal, as long as there are enough snacks out for the guests, from crunchy, pungent pickled chiles aromatic with oregano and bay leaves to crispy little fried *taquitos* served with lashings of guacamole, Cotija cheese, and *crema*, Mexico's sour cream. One master of the art of party-worthy appetizers is Alfredo Gavaldón, a Mexico City–based painter and son of the late Roberto Gavaldón, renowned Mexican cinema director. The younger Gavaldón is the kind of dignified man who can and does wear an ascot with panache. Arrive at a cocktail party in his loftlike apartment and Bach cello suites are playing, the tequila is flowing, and a serving bowl full of homemade *salpicón* and a tall stack of tostadas are on the table.

"*Salpicón* is so practical and chic, don't you think?" Gavaldón remarks, and who could disagree? His snack centerpiece has a lot of pizzazz: shredded flank steak seasoned with freshly squeezed lime juice, onion, and smoky, spicy chipotle chiles. Dressed to the nines, his guests chat among themselves as, with impeccable comportment, they spoon the steak salad onto tostadas, then squeeze lime juice on top. *Salpicón* is an ideal party food—and a classic Mexican starter.

The recipes in this chapter are some of Mexico City's most popular. Whether served at a *fonda* on a weekday, at a cantina to soak up an evening's worth of mezcal, or at a celebratory gathering, a well-prepared appetizer fires up the senses for the meal to follow. Begin, if you like, with something familiar, like guacamole with homemade tortilla chips. Or try your hand at something that might be new to you but will soon become a dish you'll want to make all the time, like garlic soup with chicken broth and paprika, tailor-made to be accompanied by beer.

This photo: The Palacio Nacional in Mexico City is the seat of the federal government. Page 30: Street eating at covered stalls, like this one near Sonora Market, makes for a quick and delicious meal.

Chilango Alfresco

Traditional Mexican food is prepared slowly, but fast-paced *chilangos*—what we residents of Mexico City call ourselves—can devour a full meal in minutes in the open air. Visitors always remark on our ability to eat standing up. Buying food from street vendors is a practice that goes back centuries; an illustration in pre-Hispanic codices depicts a woman selling a bowl of broth.

These days, food carts are usually clustered at transportation hubs. They open for business bright and early, bringing pots full of tamales, *atole* (masa porridge seasoned with cinnamon), sweet breads, and coffee. Later in the morning, they offer more substantial snacks. At lunchtime, you can order virtually anything from three-course meals to crisp-fried whole fish. In the evening, *tacos al pastor* reign, along with so much more.

Eating street food is a way to engage with the deepest essence of the city. Sometimes my motivation is simple hunger, of course; other times it's that I want to slow down and have a leisurely moment—or the sight of something delicious has set off a craving. And personally, if I have to eat on the go, far better than a preprocessed meal in a takeout container is something made by hand on a comal over a wood-fired brazier, freshly prepared just for me. —*Libia Brenda, editor, writer, and cofounder of Cúmulo de Tesla, a literary collective*

Spicy Habanero Guacamole

Guacamole con Chile Habanero

Guacamole (see photograph on the cover) has near-universal appeal and is exceedingly easy to make. Any fresh, small chile can be substituted for the habanero (if extra heat is desired, leave in the seeds). Mash the ingredients with a fork, a potato masher, or with your hands. Serve with homemade *totopos* (tortilla chips).

Makes 1½ cups

2 ripe medium avocados, halved, pitted, and peeled
¼ medium white onion, minced
1 habanero chile, seeded and minced
½ cup loosely packed fresh cilantro leaves, minced
1 to 1½ tablespoons freshly squeezed lime juice, depending on desired tartness
Salt
Tortilla chips (page 201), for serving

In a bowl, combine the avocados, onion, chile, cilantro, 1 tablespoon of the lime juice, and ½ teaspoon salt. Mix and mash the ingredients until you have a coarse, chunky-smooth consistency. Taste and add more lime juice and salt if needed. Serve at once with the tortilla chips.

Flank Steak and Avocado Tostadas

Salpicón de Res

A boldly flavored flank steak salad served on a tostada, *salpicón* is an inviting, umami-rich combination of crisp, fresh elements. Alfredo Gavaldón, the Mexico City–based artist who inspired this recipe, serves it as a party appetizer. If you want to present it as shown in the photograph on page 23, garnish it with extra lettuce, avocados, canned chipotle chiles, and tomatoes.

Makes 20 tostadas

1 pound beef flank or skirt steak, cut into 2-inch pieces
1 medium white onion, half left whole and half thinly sliced crosswise
2 garlic cloves
Salt
2 medium Roma tomatoes, coarsely chopped
2 ripe medium avocados, halved, pitted, and peeled, and cut into 1-inch cubes
2 romaine lettuce leaves, coarsely chopped
½ cup loosely packed fresh cilantro leaves, chopped
1 (2-ounce) can chipotle chiles, coarsely chopped with sauce
2 tablespoons extra-virgin olive oil
1 tablespoon red wine or cider vinegar
1 tablespoon freshly squeezed lime juice
1 teaspoon dried oregano, crumbled
Twenty 6-inch tostadas (page 202)
A few limes, quartered, for serving

1 In a pot, combine the meat, the whole onion half, the garlic, 1 teaspoon salt, and water to cover by about 2 inches. Bring to a boil, immediately turn down the heat to medium-low, cover partially, and simmer until the meat is very tender, 2 to 2½ hours. Add water as needed to maintain the original level. Remove the meat and set it aside to cool. Discard the onion, garlic, and cooking liquid.

2 Using your fingers or two forks, very finely shred the cooled meat, following the grain. Put the meat into a large serving bowl and add the tomatoes, thinly sliced onion, avocados, lettuce, cilantro, chipotles and their sauce, oil, vinegar, lime juice, oregano, and 1 teaspoon salt. Mix well, then taste for salt and add more if needed.

3 Serve the salpicón with the tostadas and limes, inviting diners to top their tostadas with a few spoonfuls of salpicón and a squeeze of lime juice.

Fava Bean and Nopales Soup (page 34).

Pasta with Shrimp and Árbol Chiles

Pasta con Camarones

Juicy with tomatoes, this pasta dish (see photograph, page 25) is light yet hearty, with depth of flavor from potent árbol chiles. It's based on a recipe from Gabriela Cámara of Contramar, the greatest of Mexico City's seafood restaurants.

Serves 4 as a first course, or 2 as a main course
- Salt
- 8 ounces dried long pasta (such as fettuccine or spaghetti)
- 5 tablespoons extra-virgin olive oil
- ¼ medium white onion, minced
- 2 garlic cloves, minced
- 1 to 2 dried árbol chiles, cut into ¼-inch pieces
- 6 medium Roma tomatoes, minced (about 2 cups)
- 12 ounces medium shrimp, peeled and deveined
- 3 tablespoons fresh basil leaves, coarsely chopped
- ½ cup finely crumbled Cotija (see page 193) or coarse-grated Pecorino Romano cheese

1 Bring a large pot of salted water to a boil. Add the pasta and cook until just al dente, according to package directions. Drain and set aside.

2 Heat a 12-inch skillet over medium heat. When the pan is hot, add 4 tablespoons of the oil. When the oil is hot, add the onion and cook, stirring often, until translucent, about 5 minutes. Add the garlic and chiles and cook, stirring, until the garlic softens, about 3 minutes; don't let the garlic turn too golden. Add the tomatoes and ½ teaspoon salt and cook, stirring occasionally, until most of their liquid has evaporated, about 10 minutes.

3 Raise the heat slightly, add the shrimp, and cook, stirring occasionally, until the shrimp are opaque and pink, about 6 minutes. Taste for salt and add if needed. Add the cooked pasta and the remaining 1 tablespoon oil and combine well. Transfer the pasta to individual bowls, top with the basil and cheese, and serve immediately.

Fava Bean and Nopales Soup

Sopa de Habas con Nopales

In this soup (see photograph, page 33), spearmint, a traditional Mexican companion to fava beans, adds nuance. If you cannot find nopales, coarsely chopped green beans can be substituted.

Serves 4
- 2 cups dried peeled yellow fava beans (see page 192), rinsed
- 2 spearmint or peppermint sprigs
- 9 cups water
- 2 cups cubed cleaned nopales (see page 202), in ½-inch cubes (about 7 ounces)
- Salt
- 5 tablespoons canola oil
- ½ medium white onion, finely chopped
- 2 medium Roma tomatoes, finely chopped
- 5 cilantro sprigs
- 2 pasilla chiles

1 In a medium pot, combine the fava beans, mint, and water and bring to a boil, skimming off any foam that forms. Turn down the heat to medium, cover partially, and cook, stirring occasionally, until the beans are beginning to fall apart, 1½ to 2 hours. If the water level falls to expose the tops of the beans, add more boiling water, ½ cup at a time, as needed to cover. When the favas are ready, remove from the heat and, using the back of a large spoon, mash the beans until somewhat smooth. Set aside.

2 Meanwhile, prepare the nopales. Bring a medium saucepan filled with water to a boil. Add the nopales and ½ teaspoon salt, turn down the heat to medium, and cook until tender, about 5 minutes. Drain them, then rinse thoroughly with cold running water to remove some of their slimy juice. Set the nopales aside.

Clockwise from top left: Lentil Soup with Bacon and Cilantro (page 37); Drunken Rice (page 37); Cantina-Style Garlic Soup (page 39); Traditional Bean Dip with Fresh Corn (page 39).

3 In another medium saucepan, heat 2 tablespoons of the oil over medium heat. When the oil is hot, add the onion and cook, stirring constantly, until translucent and just turning golden, about 4 minutes. Add the tomatoes and cook, stirring, until they begin to soften, about 3 minutes. Add the cilantro, nopales, and the cooked beans, including all of their liquid, and 2 teaspoons salt. The mixture should be the consistency of soup. If it's too dry, add water, ½ cup at a time. Mix well, then taste for salt, adding more if needed. Simmer gently for 30 minutes.

4 Meanwhile, line a plate with a paper towel. Heat a skillet over medium heat. When the pan is hot, add the remaining 3 tablespoons oil. When the oil is hot, add the chiles and fry on all sides until they are slightly puffy and about 2 shades darker, about 3 minutes. Transfer to the lined plate.

5 Ladle the soup into individual bowls. Stem the chiles and julienne them, with their seeds, then sprinkle them on each serving. Or invite diners to break the whole chiles into small pieces directly into their soup. Serve immediately.

Lentil Soup with Bacon and Cilantro

Sopa de Lentejas con Tocino

Lentil soup seasoned with bacon (see photograph, page 35, top left) is a Mexico City staple, with every *fonda* offering it at least weekly. If you like, add a dollop of Tomatillo Salsa (page 201) and offer warm tortillas at the table.

Serves 4

    ⅓ medium white onion, thickly sliced
    1 garlic clove, halved
    2 medium Roma tomatoes, thickly sliced
    6 cups water
    4 slices bacon (about 4 ounces), cut into
        1-inch-wide pieces

A cook at a traditional restaurant called a fonda.

    1 cup small or regular brown lentils
        (see page 192), rinsed
    10 cilantro sprigs
    Salt

1 In a blender, combine the onion, garlic, tomatoes, and 3 cups of the water and blend until smooth. Set aside.

2 Heat a large saucepan over medium heat. When the pan is hot, add the bacon and cook, stirring often, until the fat is nearly fully rendered, about 5 minutes. Mix in the lentils, then add the tomato mixture and stir well. Add the cilantro, turn up the heat, and bring the mixture to a boil. Turn down the heat to low, cover partially, and cook, stirring occasionally, until the mixture reduces by roughly half, about 30 minutes.

3 Add the remaining 3 cups water and ½ teaspoon salt and stir well. Re-cover partially and simmer until the lentils are tender but not breaking apart, about 40 minutes depending on the size of the lentils. Add water as needed to maintain a soupy consistency. Taste for salt, adding more if needed.

Drunken Rice

Arroz Borracho

In a country known for superior rice dishes, *arroz borracho* (see photograph, page 35, top right) is a standout recipe. Layered with flavor, it makes a good side dish, too, pairing well with nearly anything soupy. Although medium-grain rice is traditional, jasmine rice yields a reliably excellent result.

Serves 4

    1 cup jasmine rice
    2½ tablespoons canola oil
    ⅓ medium red onion, coarsely chopped
    1 garlic clove, bruised
    ½ cup water
    1 small Roma tomato, coarsely chopped
    1 small carrot, peeled and cut into tiny cubes
        (about ½ cup)

¾ cup crisp, light beer
3 cilantro sprigs
Salt

1 Rinse the rice in a fine-mesh sieve under cold running water, massaging the rice until the water runs clear.

2 Heat a saucepan over medium-high heat. When the saucepan is hot, add 1 tablespoon of the oil. When the oil is hot, add the onion and garlic and cook, stirring often, until softened and just picking up golden spots, about 4 minutes. Remove from the heat and transfer the onions and garlic to a blender.

3 To the blender, add the water and tomato and blend to a smooth liquid. Strain through a fine-mesh sieve into a bowl and discard the solids.

4 Return the saucepan to medium-high heat. When the pan is hot, add the remaining 1½ tablespoons oil. When the oil is hot, add the rice and cook, stirring often, until it just starts to turn golden, about 5 minutes. Add the blended vegetable liquid and the carrot and cook, uncovered, until the rice has absorbed nearly all of the liquid, about 3 minutes. Stir in the beer, cilantro, and ½ to 1 teaspoon salt and cook just until the liquid comes to a boil. Cover tightly, turn down the heat as low as possible, and cook for 10 minutes. Stir the rice, re-cover, and allow the rice to cook for 5 minutes longer.

5 Remove from the heat, fluff with a fork, and let rest uncovered, for 10 minutes before serving.

Pickled Chiles and Vegetables with Thyme, Oregano, and Bay Leaves
Chiles en Vinagre

Eat these vegetables (see photograph, page 20) and their pickling juice as you would a salsa. Use the smallest potatoes you can find. Packed into clean glass jars, this will keep in the refrigerator for up to 2 months. If you find fresh green árbol chiles, throw in a handful.

Makes about 5 pints

About 10 large or 15 medium jalapeño chiles, stems intact (about 1 pound)
About 15 large serrano chiles, stems intact (about 6 ounces)
8 cups water
2 medium white onions, each cut into eighths
2 medium carrots, peeled and cut into ⅓-inch-thick coins (about 1 cup)
2 cups small cauliflower florets
1½ cups very small white or red potatoes, no larger than 1 inch diameter, halved (or small white or red potatoes, quartered)
1 cup garlic cloves, peeled
20 whole allspice berries
8 bay leaves
2 teaspoons dried thyme
2 tablespoons dried oregano
Salt
1¾ cups cider or white wine vinegar
½ cup extra-virgin olive oil

1 Using the tip of a knife, poke two small holes into each chile. In a large pot, combine the water, chiles, onions, carrots, cauliflower, potatoes, garlic, allspice, bay leaves, thyme, oregano, and 3 tablespoons salt and bring to a boil. Turn down the heat and cook, uncovered, at a lively simmer, occasionally submerging the chiles, until the chiles are just fork-tender, 20 to 25 minutes.

2 Add the vinegar and stir well, then taste for salt, adding more if needed. Cook until the chiles are tender and their tops are wrinkled, 15 to 20 minutes longer. Taste again for salt. Add the oil, stir well, and remove from the heat. Bring to room temperature.

3 This can be eaten the same day, but the flavor will intensify over time. To store, transfer the vegetables and their liquid to glass jars, cap tightly, and refrigerate.

Cantina-Style Garlic Soup

Sopa de Ajo

This is a classic cantina soup (see photograph, page 35, bottom right) for good reason: it pairs well with beer, tequila, mezcal, or a tannic white wine.

Serves 4

  5 tablespoons olive oil
  1½ heads garlic (20 to 25 cloves), separated into
      cloves, peeled, and coarsely chopped
  1 medium Roma tomato, coarsely chopped
  2 cilantro sprigs
  1½ teaspoons sweet paprika
  4 cups Mexican chicken broth (page 194)
  Salt
  4 baguette slices, each ⅓ inch thick
  4 very thin slices Manchego (see page 194),
      Monterey Jack, or other good melting cheese

1 In a small skillet, heat 3 tablespoons of the oil over low heat. Add the garlic, cover, and cook, stirring often, until golden and softened, about 15 minutes (don't let the garlic brown). Raise the heat slightly and add the tomato, cilantro, and paprika and cook, stirring often, until the tomato just begins to soften, about 3 minutes. Remove from the heat, pour into a blender, add 1 cup of the broth, and blend until smooth.

2 Pour the broth mixture into a medium saucepan and add the remaining 3 cups broth. Taste for salt, adding more if needed. Bring to a simmer and cook on low heat for 10 minutes.

3 Wipe out the skillet, place over medium heat, and add the remaining 2 tablespoons oil. When the oil is hot, add the baguette slices and fry both sides until golden, 2 to 3 minutes total. Top each baguette slice with a cheese slice, flip them cheese-side down, and cook until the cheese is melted and golden, about 1 minute.

4 Ladle the soup into individual bowls and top each serving with a cheese crouton. Serve immediately.

Traditional Bean Dip with Fresh Corn

Frijoles de la Casa

Refried beans (see photograph, page 35, bottom left) makes for a popular dip in Mexico City. This version with corn is kicky with onion and garlic. It can be made from any cooked beans, though *frijoles peruanos* are traditional. Eat it with abandon, served with tortilla chips or tostadas.

Makes 3 cups

  3 tablespoons pork lard (see page 199) or
      canola oil
  ¾ cup finely chopped white onion
  3 garlic cloves, finely chopped
  Kernels from 2 ears corn
  2½ cups cooked beans with their cooking liquid
      (see Mexican-Style Stewed Beans, page 192)
  Salt
  1 cup coarsely crumbled Cojita (see page 193) or
      coarse-grated Pecorino Romano cheese
  Tortilla chips (page 201) or tostadas (page 202),
      for serving

1 In a large skillet, heat the lard over medium-low heat. Add the onion, garlic, and corn and cook, stirring often, until the onion and garlic are golden, 15 to 20 minutes.

2 Add the beans and their liquid and, using a masher or the back of a spoon, mash the beans until they're the consistency of chunky peanut butter. If the mixture is too dry, add warm water, 1 tablespoon at a time.

3 Taste for salt, adding if needed. Transfer to a serving dish and let cool slightly. Sprinkle the cheese on top and serve with the tortilla chips.

3

Without Corn, There Is No Mexico

Foods Made from Corn

In Colonia Escandón on a Saturday morning around eleven, there's a softness in the air: shopkeepers are just opening their doors and traffic is sparse. It's less hectic than a weekday but without Sunday's usual somnolence. In a sun-dappled spot under a tree where food vendors congregate, Alejandro and Bety Nieto are setting up the mesquite-fired grill on which they'll make *tlacoyos*, oval-shaped patties—as big as your outstretched hand—made from masa (corn dough).

The Nietos live in milpa country, the agricultural fields that lie on the fringes of Mexico City. The maize, or corn, the Nietos use was once from their own farm, but these days they're sourcing it from a neighbor and preparing it at home. Made from purple corn, the masa looks and smells like the primordial food that it is: a deep bluish-gray dough with an earthy scent like clean, damp stone.

Alejandro, still youthful in his forties, is the more reserved of the pair, while Bety greets customers with an amused sparkle; both have a natural grace as they take handfuls of the claylike masa and roll them into balls, which they stuff with mashed fava beans and requesón, a cheese similar to ricotta. Bety then pats the masa into the distinctive oval shape of the *tlacoyo*, and onto the grill go the first of the day. To observe the pair cook is to watch craftsmanship at play. Bety, deftly cracking the crust of the inaugural *tlacoyo*

with the tap of a finger, pauses to ask a customer what toppings he prefers before adding a spoonful of cactus salad and topping the whole with salsa and crumbled Cotija cheese. Breakfast is ready. Beneath the toasty first bite is the taste of corn, then the savory filling, fiery salsa, salty cheese. It's incredible eating. "This is what our parents did, and their parents before them, this work. Growing the maize, making *tlacoyos*, and selling them for people to enjoy," Alejandro says. "It is a good job."

It's impossible to overstate the reverence with which maize is regarded in Mexico: it is the cornerstone of the culture. According to legend, the Aztecs were originally unable to access corn because it was beyond their reach, hidden behind mountains. Their priests begged Quetzalcoatl, the serpent god, for help, whereupon he obligingly transformed himself into an ant and carried a kernel back to his people to be planted. Corn became the wellspring of their civilization.

The transformation of corn into masa has barely changed in fifty-five hundred years. The hard kernels of maize are ground, soaked, and cooked with an alkali—traditionally wood ash. This process, nixtamalization, enhances the flavor and aroma of the maize and improves its nutritional benefits. Countless prepared foods, most importantly tortillas and tamales, the mainstays of Mexican cuisine, come from the dough, or masa, made from the nixtamalized corn. Small wonder, then, that

Fresh tortillas made with white,
yellow, blue, and purple corn masa
and nopales-flavored corn masa in
a tortillería in Mercado Portales.

Wisdom of the Cornfield

The scene at left of a *milpa*, a sustainable Mexican farming practice that dates back to prehistory, could be observed every day in the rural parts of Mexico City until as recently as forty years ago; this image is from the 1920s. The tradition is a practice of crop rotation involving beans, squash, maize, herbs, and sometimes chiles that nourishes the soil without depleting it. Since soil quality affects everything from a food's nutritional value to the local ecosystem, the benefits of the milpa are inestimable, and it's a method that fosters an intimate relationship between farmers and their crops. A community disconnected from the earth hastens its own demise. Conversely, working the land affirms family ties, gives deep meaning to celebrations, and, over time, makes even death itself become less threatening. For in the milpa, there is ample proof that everything is reborn. —*Pablo Orube, Mexico City–based author, historian, and professor of cinema*

corn has passionate advocates. Although modern Mexican agricultural practices favor a single variety of high-yield hybrid white corn, a growing movement of cooks and farmers is devoted to promoting genetically diverse indigenous corn—and, along with it, a pillar of native Mexican culture. In 2013, legislation to prohibit the growing of genetically modified corn crops was passed. Although the law's efficacy is doubtful, Mexico's corn defenders remain vigilant.

This morning in Escandón, the Nietos are only two of the local vendors preparing corn-based dishes and *antojitos*, the most popular street snacks of Mexico. Just down the street, a mobile *pozolera* is being wheeled into place. Once the pot is simmering and the countertop and stools have been set up, a customer can hunker down to a steaming bowl of pozole, a rich pork stew that features hominy, or nix-tamalized whole corn kernels.

A tantalizing aroma draws crowds to an *elote preparado* vendor. *Elote* is what Americans think of as sweet corn, which here is being boiled in pots on a half dozen charcoal grills. The cook pulls each tender ear from the pot, drives a wooden skewer through its base, and coats it with mayonnaise, grated tangy aged cheese, chile powder, and lime juice. The result, with its festive appearance, is a pure celebration of this fundamental food.

Opposite: Corn on the Cob with Cheese and Chile (page 65). Page 50: Tlayuda with Chorizo and Avocado (page 66). Page 51: a scene from Centro Histórico.

A Sacred Memory One *tortillería* of my childhood was a narrow shop alive with the metallic screech of gears and pulleys. I liked to stand in view of the conveyor belt. It was hypnotic to watch the dough stretch into a sheet that the mechanical cutters made into neat rounds, then see the raw tortillas travel in an endless band, disappearing into a mysterious space above before reappearing from below, cooked. At another *tortillería*, the process was old fashioned. There, a woman placed the raw dough by hand onto a hot comal. Those were my favorite tortillas, as they were twice as big as their conveyor-belt counterparts. And while they were cooking, they would puff up as though they were flying saucers about to lift off.

—LIBIA BRENDA

Tacos al pastor, *a chipotle-marinated pork filling topped with pineapple, onions, and cilantro (page 67). The Mexican-Lebanese dish is the city's most popular style of taco.*

Taco Town *The undisputed king of Mexico City street food, tacos are on offer virtually everywhere you turn, served with condiments like salsa, guacamole, and sliced radishes. Of the myriad varieties, here are some of the most popular types.*

Home Cooking on the Go *Home-style main dishes fill a taco de guisado (below). Often there will be ten or more options to choose from, such as chicken with green mole sauce, adobo (spiced meat stew), scrambled eggs, or chile relleno.*

Barbecued, Stewed, Braised *Specialty tacos include* barbacoa de carnero, *made with pit-roasted lamb (right);* chivo, *or goat stew; or* carnitas, *Michoacán-style pork braised in lard until it is of the utmost tenderness and succulence.*

Hot Off the Grill *Follow the scent of aromatic smoke to find tacos al carbon (above): pork chops, beef, or cecina (salt-cured flank steak) grilled to order, then chopped and put directly from the flame onto a warm tortilla.*

Slow Food Served Fast
Only tacos de suadero *(right) can touch the popularity of* tacos al pastor. *Beef is braised for hours until tender with tripe and other offal, spring onions, and sometimes chorizo or longaniza, a chorizo-like sausage. The taco is topped with lime juice, cilantro, chopped onions, and salsa.*

Slow-Cooked Pork and Hominy Stew

Pozole Rojo

Venture into a public market such as La Merced and you're likely to end up encountering a bowl of pozole, a luscious stew of pork and hominy much like this one. The salad's worth of garnishes that go on top of it (oregano, radish, onion, lettuce, lime juice) makes it an ideal one-dish party food. It's brothy, so use a cut of meat that yields rich stock. This recipe calls for baby-back pork ribs, though you could use another cut of pork, preferably bone-in. Note that pozole is a true slow food: while it will technically be done at the time given below, the longer you cook it, the richer the flavor you will get.

Serves 6

5 cups cooked, drained hominy (see page 198)

5 quarts cold water

2½ pounds baby-back pork ribs, halved crosswise by the butcher if possible

1½ medium white onions, 1 whole onion halved, the remaining half finely chopped

8 garlic cloves

Salt

2 cups hot water

8 guajillo chiles, stemmed and seeded

4 bay leaves

Pinch of ground cumin

4 whole allspice berries

¼ cup plus 1½ teaspoons dried oregano

6 radishes, thinly sliced

2 cups shredded iceberg lettuce

5 limes, quartered

¼ cup piquín or cayenne chile powder

Twelve 6-inch tostadas (page 202)

1 In a colander, rinse the hominy under cold running water. In a large pot, combine the 5 quarts water, hominy, pork, whole onion halves, garlic, and 1 tablespoon salt. Bring to a rolling boil over high heat and immediately turn down the heat to medium-low. Simmer gently, stirring occasionally and skimming off any foam that forms on the surface, until the meat is falling-apart tender and the hominy has cracked open, about 2½ hours. If the liquid drops to the level of the pork and hominy, add water to cover by 1 to 2 inches.

2 Meanwhile, heat a 12-inch skillet over medium heat. While the pan is heating, pour the 2 cups hot water into a medium bowl. Add the chiles to the hot pan and heat, turning them frequently, until they are lightly toasted but not burned, about 2 minutes. Transfer the chiles to the bowl of hot water, submerging them, and let stand until completely softened, about 10 minutes.

3 With the skillet still over medium heat, add the bay leaves, cumin, allspice, and 1½ teaspoons of the oregano and cook, stirring constantly, until the herbs and spices are fragrant, about 3 minutes. Transfer the contents of the skillet to a blender, add the softened chiles and their soaking water, and blend until smooth.

4 When the hominy and meat are cooked, remove from the heat. Taste for salt and add more if needed. Scoop out the ribs and let cool until they can be handled. Discard the bones and cut or tear the meat into rough 1-inch pieces.

5 Using a fine-mesh sieve, strain the blended chile mixture into the pot of hominy and broth. Return the meat to the pot and mix well, then taste for salt and adjust if needed. Cook over medium-low heat, stirring occasionally, until all of the ingredients have integrated and the flavors are blended, about 30 minutes. Remove from the heat and let stand for about 15 minutes before serving.

6 Set out the remaining ¼ cup oregano, the radishes, chopped onion, lettuce, limes, and chile powder in separate small bowls on the table. Ladle the pozole into individual bowls and serve. Invite diners to add the garnishes to their bowls as desired—and serve with tostadas.

A young girl holds a plate of Fava Bean–Stuffed Masa Cakes (page 68).

Cheese Quesadillas

Quesadillas de Queso

The key to perfect quesadillas (see photograph, page 18) is fresh, quality tortillas and a good melting cheese, such as Manchego or quesillo (see page 194). But you can use any cheese you love that has excellent melting properties— perhaps Comté or a good Cheddar—and you can also explore possible traditional additions, such as cooked poblano chiles (see Variation). Serve them hot off the pan accompanied by freshly made salsa, such as the Grilled Tomato and Green Chile Salsa on page 200. To make these quesadillas into a meal, accompany them with Mexican-Style Stewed Beans (page 192).

Makes 6 quesadillas

5 tablespoons canola oil

Six 6-inch corn tortillas, homemade (page 196) or store-bought

1 cup pulled quesillo or other string cheese (in thin strips), grated Manchego, or other grated good melting cheese

Heat a comal or large skillet over medium heat. When the pan is hot, add 1 tablespoon of the oil. When the oil is hot, add as many tortillas as will easily fit in the pan in a single layer. Heat the tortillas on one side, pressing with a spatula, until hot and flexible, about 30 seconds; add more oil if needed. Flip the tortillas over, add 2 to 3 tablespoons cheese on half of each tortilla, immediately fold over the uncovered half, and press down on the folded tortillas until the underside is beginning to pick up golden spots, about 2 minutes. Flip the tortillas and keep pressing with the spatula until cheese starts to ooze out of the sides and some crunchy spots have formed on the underside, another minute or two. Transfer to a plate. Repeat with the remaining tortillas and cheese. Serve hot.

Chile Variation: Generally, a poblano chile is roasted before using, but in this case, it's sautéed. For six quesadillas, heat a medium skillet over medium-low heat and add 1 tablespoon oil. When the oil is hot, add ¼ medium white onion, thinly sliced, and 1 poblano chile, stemmed, seeded, and cut into narrow 2-inch-long strips. Cook, stirring occasionally, just until the onion and chile are softened, about 15 minutes. Season to taste with salt, add ¼ cup coarsely chopped fresh epazote leaves (optional; see page 198), and cook just until the leaves wilt. Add this mixture to the tortillas after you add the cheese, dividing it evenly among the six quesadillas.

Crisp-Fried Taco Flutes

Taquitos

Taquito literally means "little taco," but it's understood to signify a taco that is rolled into a tight cylinder and fried. These crunchy tortillas (see photograph, page 19) are stuffed with chicken, though you can fill them with other savory mixtures, from refried beans (page 193) to leftover *salpicón* (page 32) to mashed potatoes and cooked poblano chile strips. For an appetizer or a fun children's meal, serve them with plenty of toppings, as is done here.

Makes 15 taquitos; serves 5

2 cups Shredded Poached Chicken Breast (page 195)

Fifteen 6-inch corn tortillas, homemade (page 196) or store-bought, at room temperature

Canola oil, for frying

1 cup crema (see page 196)

2 cups finely shredded iceberg lettuce

1½ cups Grilled Tomato and Green Chile Salsa (page 200)

½ cup finely crumbled Cotija (see page 193) or coarse-grated Pecorino Romano cheese

The pedestrian promenade Avenida Madero in Centro Histórico.

Tortillas a Mano

Making tortillas from scratch and by hand—the traditional method—is an excellent way to understand this staple food, and is a truly Mexican approach. Note that homemade tortillas turn out thicker and less uniform than tortillas made in a press or store-bought (see page 196). First, you make masa by pouring dried maize into a pot with an alkali substance and water (opposite, top left). This mixture simmers until the corn is partially cooked. Leave the corn to soak and cool, then rinse, drain, and grind it until it forms masa, or dough. With moistened hands, knead the masa vigorously, turning it and slapping it frequently to introduce a little air (top right). Set aside a smaller portion of masa (middle left); it should be between damp and dry: slightly tacky to the touch but not wet, with edges that hold together without cracking. With your hands, shape a few tablespoons of the masa into a disk (middle right). Then, in a circular motion, pat it into a tortilla shape (bottom left). Place the tortilla onto a hot comal (bottom right). The side that first touches the comal is known as the *piel* ("skin") side. Cook until the top looks slightly dry and the bottom releases readily from the pan. Flip the tortilla over and cook it on the other side. When it puffs up and the bottom has picked up toasty golden spots, it's ready to eat.

1 Place about 2 tablespoons of the chicken in the center of a tortilla and roll up the tortilla into the tightest possible cylinder, taking care not to break it. Transfer the taquito, seam side down, to a large plate. Repeat with the remaining tortillas and chicken, placing the taquitos close together so they retain their shape. Cover with a clean kitchen towel to keep them moist.

2 Line a large plate with paper towels. Heat a 12-inch skillet over medium-high heat and pour in the oil to a depth of ⅓ inch. When the oil is hot (to test it, drop in a small scrap of tortilla; if bubbles form around it instantly, the oil is ready), place a taquito, seam side down, into the pan and, using a spatula, immediately hold it in place until the edges are sealed together, about 30 seconds. Add a few more taquitos and seal the same way. They will hold their shape better if the sides of the taquitos are touching—a toothpick inserted in the center of each will help them stay closed. Cook the taquitos, turning them as needed, until golden on all sides, about 3 minutes total. Using tongs, transfer the taquitos to the towel-lined plate to drain. Repeat with the remaining taquitos, adding more oil to the pan as needed.

3 To serve, arrange three taquitos on each individual plate and garnish each serving with a generous tablespoon each of crema, lettuce, salsa, and cheese.

Tamales Stuffed with Refried Beans
Tamales de Frijol

Tamales (see photograph, page 40), cakes of masa wrapped in corn husks and then steamed until tender, are prepared in any number of ways, depending on the region from which they come. This classic recipe comes from Martha Alvarez Cordero, who lives in Milpa Alta, where cityscape gives way to farmland. Petite and fluffy—the pork lard creates a light, moist texture—these tamales are stuffed with refried beans to which aromatic avocado leaves can be

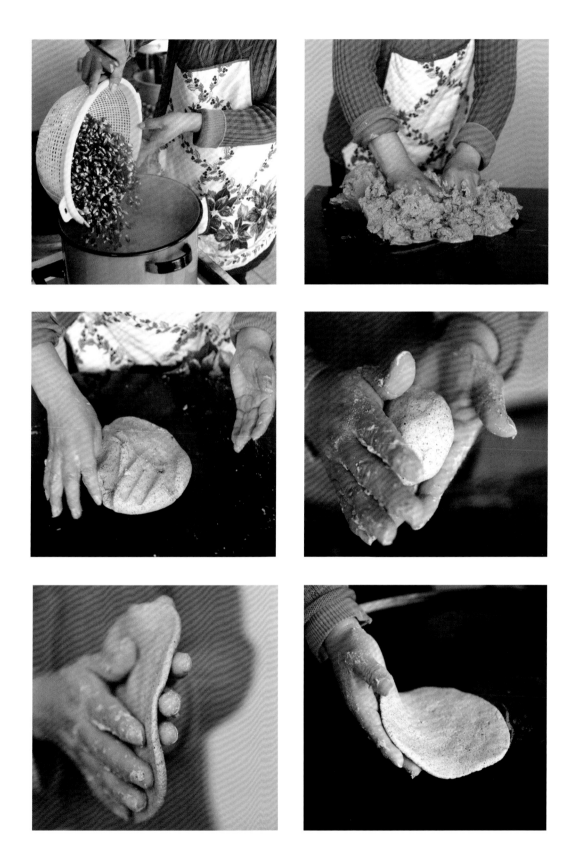

added. They are typically eaten slathered with mole sauce (use the recipe on page 138, minus the chicken), but they really don't need any more than a dab of Grilled Tomato and Green Chile Salsa (page 200) and a drizzle of crema (see page 196). Note that the beans must be prepared at least 3 hours in advance of assembling the tamales; the dried corn husks (available at Mexican specialty shops) will need to soak for 1 hour before wrapping the tamales.

Makes about 20 small tamales

   About 40 dried corn husks
   6 cups (3 pounds) fresh homemade masa
      (page 199) or store-bought,
      at room temperature
   ¾ cup pork lard (see page 199),
      at room temperature
   Salt
   1½ cups refried beans (page 193)

1 At least 1 hour before you are ready to wrap the tamales, soak the dried corn husks in water to cover for 1 hour, then drain them.

2 Put the masa into a large bowl and knead it until it is light in texture, about 5 minutes. If it becomes stiff or dry, add warm water, 1 tablespoon at a time. Add half of the lard (6 tablespoons) and ½ teaspoon salt and knead until the lard is well incorporated and the masa is soft and pliant, about 3 minutes. Add the remaining lard and another ½ teaspoon salt and knead until fully incorporated. Taste for salt and add more if needed.

3 To make each tamale, hold a corn husk with the rounded end sitting in the cup of your hand, its pointy end facing away. Spoon 3 heaping tablespoons of masa onto the husk and spread the masa until it covers a space about the size of your hand and is about ⅓ inch thick. Add 1 tablespoon of the beans to the center of the masa. Fold over the left side of the husk until it covers all of the stuffing. Fold over the right side of the husk the same way, then roll from the right side until the tamale is secure and tightly wrapped. Fold the pointed end of the corn husk over, then press it gently down. Repeat until you have used all of the masa and bean stuffing. Some husks may not be large enough to encase the masa and filling, so you may need to use two husks.

4 To steam the tamales, pour water to a depth of about 1 inch into a 12-quart *tamalera* (see page 197) or a stockpot with a colander set on the bottom. If you like, place a coin on the bottom of the pot, which will rattle as the water bubbles. If the water runs dry, the coin will go silent, alerting you to add more water. Crumple ten soaked corn husks and use them to make a bed on the steamer rack or colander. This prevents the boiling water from penetrating the tamales. Arrange the tamales upright in the pot, with their rounded ends resting on the rack or colander. Crumple any remaining corn husks and use to cover the tamales. Turn the heat to high and cover the pot. When you hear a rattling sound—a sign the water is boiling—turn down the heat to medium and steam the tamales until they are cooked, 1 hour and 25 minutes. Check once or twice to be sure there's still water in the pot (or listen for the sound of the rattling coin). To test if the tamales are ready, remove one from the pot, let it rest for a minute or two, then open it. The masa should appear cooked and should easily pull away from the husk.

5 Remove the tamales from the steamer and serve hot. What you don't eat right away you can store, tightly covered, in the refrigerator for up to 1 week. They reheat well in a microwave or in a steamer.

Corn on the Cob with Cheese and Chile

Elote Preparado

When it comes to snack food in Mexico City, *elote preparado* (see photograph, page 48) rules the streets. Consisting of corn on the cob served on a kebab stick and coated with mayonnaise, Cotija cheese, chile powder, and lime juice, it's as fun to eat as it is delicious. This recipe epitomizes two core aspects of Mexican cooking: flamboyance and festivity.

Serves 4

    4 large ears yellow or white corn,
        husked and stem cut off
    Salt
    About ¾ cup mayonnaise
    About ¾ cup finely crumbled Cotija
        (see page 193) or coarse-grated
        Pecorino Romano cheese
    About 1 tablespoon piquín or cayenne
        chile powder (optional)
    A few limes, quartered

1 In a pot large enough to hold all of the corn, combine the corn, 1½ teaspoons salt, and water to cover generously and bring to a rolling boil over high heat. Taste the water; it should be as salty as sea water. Add more salt if needed. Turn down the heat to medium, cover, and cook until the corn is very tender when pierced with a fork, about 20 minutes. Drain the corn.

2 Have ready four kebab sticks each thick enough to support an ear of corn. While the corn is still warm but has cooled enough to touch, insert a kebab stick through the stem end down the center of each ear. Holding each ear by its stick, completely slather the ear with a generous quantity of the mayonnaise (at least a tablespoon). Next, sprinkle the cheese over the ear, covering it evenly; a little less than ¼ cup should be sufficient. Then, evenly sprinkle the ear with a few generous pinches of chile powder, if using. Finally, squeeze lime juice liberally over each ear. Serve at once.

The Corn Deity

Maize—corn to Americans—has a vital place in Mexican culture. It is food, of course, but it is also a powerful entity, engendering devotion that transcends regional identity. Historically, it has had several spiritual manifestations. The Toltec people of ancient Mesoamerica named this deity Centéotl. This god was adopted by the Mexicas (later known as the Aztecs), who endowed it with qualities particular to their religion, such as having dual genders; their Centéotl was also the patron of drunkenness and ritual beverages. S/he was particularly revered because having made the sacrifice to live under the earth was an act of generosity that gave humanity the treasure of maize. Without it, there would be no nation, indeed no people. It is no exaggeration to say that maize is not only a nourishing food but also a divine gift. —*Pablo Orube*

Tlayuda with Chorizo and Avocado
Tlayuda con Chorizo y Aguacate

A *tlayuda* (see photograph, page 50) is a thin round of toasted masa dough about the size of a pizza, which is covered with toppings and then grilled until it is crunchy and has a primal, fireside flavor. *Tlayudas*—a specialty of the state of Oaxaca—are not readily available outside of Mexico, so you may not find them in the Mexican food shops in your area. You can substitute four 6-inch corn tostadas, though, and divide the toppings among them. This rendition was provided by chef Alam Méndez Florián of Mexico City's Pasillo de Humo restaurant, which serves contemporary stylings of traditional Oaxacan food. It calls for string cheese and chorizo and adds an untraditional salad-like topping of tart, crisp purslane, to raise street food into something sublime.

Serves 2 as a main course

⅛ medium red onion, sliced lengthwise paper-thin

1 chile güero encurtido (see page 195) or 2 pepperoncini, stemmed and thinly sliced

1 tablespoon freshly squeezed lime juice

Salt

One 15-inch tlayuda or four 6-inch tostadas (page 202)

¾ cup pulled quesillo (see page 194) or other string cheese, in thin strips

1 tablespoon olive oil, plus more if needed

7 tablespoons fresh Mexican chorizo (see page 196), casing discarded

1 cup purslane leaves (see page 202), most stems discarded, dried well after rinsing (optional)

¾ cup cubed ripe avocado (in 1-inch cubes)

1 Preheat the oven to 400°F. In a small bowl, combine the onion, chile, lime juice, and a pinch of salt and mix well. Set aside to marinate at room temperature for 15 minutes.

Unlocking the Flavor

Food in Mexico City was originally prepared by cooking directly on red-hot embers or, later, on a wood-fired *fogón* (stove). Long after that, rustic equipment was supplanted by gas ranges in many urban dwellings, though rural home cooks continued to prepare dishes in the same manner their ancestors did, at a slow simmer over low heat. And there's a reason for that: slow cooking yields a depth of flavor that cannot be matched by any other means. Some Mexican dishes, such as quick-fried *taquitos*, are meant to be prepared with speed. And some recipes call for charring, searing, or browning an ingredient quickly over a high flame to ready it for a longer, slower cooking process. But by and large, the approach is deliberate, done with care and attention.

The steps follow a pattern. Heat the pan before adding the cooking fat; when the fat is hot, add the ingredients in a specific order, and then wait patiently while they simmer over moderate heat. In time, layers of flavor unfold in the dish, as each ingredient develops fullness and complexity. This unhurried technique is at odds with the fashion for cutting cooking time down to a bare minimum whenever possible. It is a method that takes some patience, but the payoff will be Mexican food that tastes truly Mexican.

2 Put the tlayuda or tostadas on a sheet pan and place into the preheated oven for 5 minutes. Remove from the oven and arrange the cheese evenly on top. Leave the oven on.

3 Heat a 12-inch skillet over medium heat. When the pan is hot, add the 1 tablespoon oil and chorizo and cook, stirring often and breaking up the meat with a spatula, until the chorizo renders all of its fat and the meat is golden and crumbly, about 5 minutes; add more oil if needed to prevent scorching. Remove from the heat and spread the chorizo and its fat evenly over the cheese.

4 Return the tlayuda or tostadas to the oven and cook until the cheese is fully melted, about 5 minutes. Remove from the oven and transfer to a serving platter.

5 Working quickly, in a bowl, toss together the purslane (if using) and the onion-chile mixture, then distribute the dressed purslane evenly atop the tlayuda or tostadas. (If not using the purslane, distribute the onion-chile mixture evenly over the top.) Scatter the avocado over the surface.

6 Serve at once. A tlayuda is traditionally served broken into pieces; tostadas are eaten whole.

Chipotle-Marinated Pork Tacos
Tacos al Pastor

Dominating the taco scene is *al pastor*: monumental inverted cones of marinated pork, some weighing in at over one hundred pounds, topped with a whole pineapple and licked by open flames. It's a method of seasoning and cooking meat that was popularized by Lebanese immigrants, adapted from their native *shawarma* (spit-roasted meat). This recipe comes as close to the taste of real *al pastor* as you can get at home. It calls for marinating thin slices of pork (ask your butcher to slice it, if you like) in a wealth of spices, chiles, oregano, and vinegar before frying

it, chopping it, and serving it in a hot tortilla. A key though optional ingredient is achiote paste, made from the red seeds of the achiote tree. Popular in the cooking of southeast Mexico, it is sold in blocks of a few ounces in Hispanic shops; El Yucateco is a good brand. To achieve the authentic depth of flavor, the pork must marinate for at least 3 hours, though overnight is preferable. This recipe yields a lot of meat. If you like, you can keep some of the marinated meat in an airtight container in the refrigerator for up to 4 days before cooking it. Use the pork for making tacos as detailed here, or leave the slices whole and eat as you would a cutlet, with Mexican-Style Stewed Beans (page 192), rice, and a salad.

Makes about 20 tacos

4 tablespoons canola oil, plus more as needed

5 garlic cloves

1½ medium white onions, whole onion thickly sliced crosswise and onion half finely chopped

5 bay leaves

6 guajillo chiles, stemmed and seeded

⅓ to ⅔ cup water

¼ cup cider vinegar

4 whole allspice berries

10 peppercorns

5 whole cloves

1 tablespoon dried oregano

1½ teaspoons ground ginger

1 teaspoon cumin seeds

2 tablespoons achiote paste (optional)

3 canned chipotle chiles (see page 195)

Salt

2½ pounds boneless pork loin or leg

1 cup loosely packed fresh cilantro leaves, minced

About 4 limes, quartered, for serving

Grilled Tomato and Green Chile Salsa (page 200), for serving

About twenty 6-inch corn tortillas, homemade (page 196) or store-bought, warmed

¼ large pineapple, peeled, cored, and finely diced

1 At least 4 hours before serving, make the marinade. Heat a skillet over medium heat and add 2 tablespoons of the oil. When the oil is hot, add the garlic, the sliced onion, and the bay leaves and cook, stirring occasionally, until the onion is translucent and is picking up golden spots, about 5 minutes. Add the guajillo chiles and cook, stirring occasionally, until they soften slightly and begin to smell fragrant, about 2 minutes. Add ⅓ cup of the water and the vinegar, turn down the heat to low, cover, and simmer until the chiles are fully softened, about 10 minutes. Remove from the heat.

2 In a spice grinder or with a mortar and pestle, combine the allspice, peppercorns, cloves, oregano, ginger, and cumin and grind until fully pulverized. Transfer the ground mixture to a blender, add the achiote paste (if using), chipotle chiles, 2 teaspoons salt, and the contents of the skillet, and blend until very smooth. The mixture should be the consistency of a milkshake. If it is too thick, add up to ⅓ cup water, 1 tablespoon at a time. Taste for salt. Set aside.

3 Do not trim any fat from the pork. Using a sharp knife, slice the pork against the grain as thinly as possible (about ¼ inch thick). Coat each slice with the marinade, making sure it is fully covered and stacking the slices in a glass container as they are ready. Cover the container with plastic wrap and marinate the pork for at least 3 hours or preferably overnight. About 30 minutes before you are ready to cook the pork, bring it to room temperature.

4 Heat a large nonstick skillet over medium-high heat and add 2 tablespoons of the oil. When the oil is very hot, arrange as many marinade-slathered pork slices as will fit in a single layer in the pan without crowding. Fry the slices until they have picked up appealing golden spots on the underside, 3 to 5 minutes. Flip the slices and cook until golden spots appear on the second side, 2 to 4 minutes. Transfer to a plate. Repeat with the remaining pork, adding more oil to the pan as needed.

5 While the pork is cooking, put the chopped onion, cilantro, limes, and salsa in small separate bowls and set the bowls on the table. When all of the pork is cooked, cut the slices into thin strips. Spoon the pork onto the hot tortillas, top with the pineapple, and serve at once. Invite diners to garnish their tacos as they like.

Fava Bean–Stuffed Masa Cakes
Tlacoyos

Chewy and slightly crisp on the outside, a *tlacoyo* (see photograph, page 59) is an oval masa patty stuffed with a savory filling—in this case, mashed fava beans aromatic with spearmint. Salsa roja, Cojita cheese, and cactus salad are the typical toppings. You will need to have the fava beans ready in advance, so plan accordingly. At least 3 hours before you make the tlacoyos, begin cooking the fava beans, and then set the cooked mashed fava beans aside to cool. Tlacoyos make an excellent snack or main course, and they will keep, ungarnished, in the refrigerator for up to 1 week. Reheat them in a skillet and garnish just before serving.

Makes 10 tlacoyos; serves 5

    3 cups (1½ pounds), fresh homemade
        masa (page 199) or store-bought,
        at room temperature
    Salt
    About 1 cup mashed fava beans with mint
        (see Mexican-Style Stewed Beans,
        fava bean variation, page 192)
    Canola oil, for brushing
    Cactus and Mint Salad (page 90), for garnish
        (optional)
    Grilled Tomato and Green Chile Salsa
        (page 200), for garnish

Yolanda Segura López, a home cook, presents a plate of Miners' Enchiladas (page 70).

About ½ cup finely crumbled Cotija
(see page 193) or coarse-grated Pecorino
Romano cheese

1 Put the masa into a large bowl, add 1 teaspoon salt, and, with moistened hands, knead the masa until it is smooth and pliant, about 5 minutes. If it becomes stiff or dry, add water, 1 tablespoon at a time, until the masa is more workable. Taste for salt and add more if needed.

2 Measure 3 tablespoons masa and shape it into a flat oval about 2 inches wide by 5 inches long. Using your fingers, make a slight indentation in the center. Place 1 generous tablespoon of the mashed fava beans into the indentation. Pinch the masa together to create a masa seal over the fava bean paste, then smooth the seal with your fingers. Continue to shape the tlacoyo until you have a flat, smooth-surfaced oval about 3 inches wide, 6 inches long, and ⅓ inch thick. Repeat with the remaining masa and stuffing; you should have about 10 tlacoyos. Don't worry if the seal isn't complete and some filling is exposed; repair any cracks, tears, or holes with a little water, smoothing the surface.

3 Heat a 12-inch skillet or comal over medium heat. When the pan is hot, place a tlacoyo or two onto it and cook until the masa on the underside is no longer raw and begins to pick up golden spots, about 3 minutes. Flip the tlacoyo and cook on the second side the same way, about 3 minutes. Brush the exposed side with about ½ teaspoon oil, flip the tlacoyo, and cook undisturbed until the tlacoyo has become crispier on the underside, about 1 minute. Brush the exposed side with about ½ teaspoon oil, flip one more time, and cook until crispier, about 1 minute more. Transfer the tlacoyo to a plate. Repeat with the remaining tlacoyos.

4 To serve, arrange 2 tlacoyos on each individual plate. Top each with about ½ cup of the salad (if using), salsa to taste, and a generous 1 tablespoon cheese. Serve warm.

Miners' Enchiladas
Enchiladas Mineras

An enchilada is a tortilla that has been dredged in a chile sauce before being fried, stuffed, and finally topped with garnishes. Many variations exist. Here, the sauce is made from flavorful yet mild chiles, and the dish is surprisingly delicate, a quality typical of the foods of El Bajío, the largely rural region in Central Mexico where it originates (see photograph, page 69). It's a good meal for a casual Sunday afternoon, and since it is a complete meal in itself, it can stand on its own without side dishes. Pickled Chiles and Vegetables with Thyme, Oregano, and Bay Leaves (page 38) are an excellent companion to these enchiladas.

Serves 4

2 cups Shredded Poached Chicken Breast
(page 195)
1 medium Yukon Gold or other waxy
white potato
1 carrot, peeled
Salt
3 tablespoons canola oil, plus more as needed
2 ancho chiles, stemmed and seeded
7 guajillo chiles, stemmed and seeded
2 garlic cloves
½ medium white onion
2 whole cloves
2 whole allspice berries
Pinch of ground cumin
1 tablespoon cider vinegar
Twelve 6-inch corn tortillas, homemade
(page 196) or store-bought, chilled
4 romaine lettuce leaves, finely shredded
1 cup finely crumbled Cotija (see page 193)
or Pecorino Romano cheese

1 Cook the chicken as directed, using at least 3½ cups water. When the chicken is ready, transfer it to a plate, let cool, then shred finely as directed and set aside. Strain the broth and measure 2½ cups. Pour the broth into a small saucepan and set aside.

2 In a medium saucepan, combine the potato, carrot, ½ teaspoon salt, and water to cover by 2 inches. Bring to a boil over high heat and cook until the vegetables are tender, 30 to 40 minutes. Drain and let cool until they can be handled. Peel the potato, then cut the potato and carrot into ½-inch cubes. Transfer to a bowl, season to taste with salt, and set aside.

3 To make the sauce, heat a 12-inch skillet over medium heat. When the pan is hot, add 1 tablespoon of the oil. When the oil is hot, add all of the chiles and fry, turning them once, until they begin to puff up and darken slightly, about 1 minute on each side (you might have to do this in two batches). Remove from the heat. Bring the reserved broth to a boil, remove from the heat, and add the chiles, submerging them in the broth. Let stand, stirring occasionally, until they soften, about 10 minutes. Meanwhile, return the skillet to medium heat. Add the garlic and onion and cook, turning as needed, until they start picking up golden spots, about 5 minutes. Remove from the heat.

4 In a blender, combine the softened chiles and broth, cooked garlic and onion, cloves, allspice, cumin, vinegar, and 1 teaspoon salt and blend until smooth. Strain through a fine-mesh sieve into a bowl, then taste for salt and add more if needed.

5 Return the skillet to medium heat and add 1 tablespoon oil. When the oil is hot, add the strained sauce (watch out, as it will splatter) and cook, stirring often, until it has reduced by about 10 percent. Transfer the sauce to a shallow bowl.

6 Have everything ready before you start preparing the enchiladas: the chilled tortillas, the bowl of sauce, the shredded chicken, the potato-carrot mixture, the shredded lettuce, the crumbled cheese, and four individual plates. Heat a 12-inch nonstick skillet over medium heat. When the pan is hot, add 1 tablespoon oil. Using tongs, grasp one tortilla and quickly dip first one side and then the other side of the tortilla into the sauce, and then immediately transfer the doused tortilla to the pan. Cook the tortilla, using the tongs to flip it once, for 2 minutes on each side. (Some of the tortillas might tear as you try to flip them, but keep trying.) With the tortilla still in the pan, place about 2 tablespoons of the shredded chicken along the center of the tortilla, then carefully transfer the tortilla to one of the plates. Fold one side of the tortilla over the filling and then the other, turning it seam side down. Repeat with the remaining tortillas, adding additional oil to the pan as needed and putting three filled enchiladas on each plate.

7 Garnish each serving with about ½ cup of the potato-carrot mixture, followed by ¼ cup lettuce and ¼ cup cheese. Serve at once.

Nourishing Land, Nourishing Table

Vegetables

★ LO MEJOR DEL DÍA ★

$20⁰⁰
KILO

★ OFERTA ★

2 KILOS X$ 20

Opposite: Mexican-Style Stewed Zucchini and Poblanos (page 90). Page 72: flame-charred poblano chiles. Pages 74 to 75: vegetables stacked at a stall near Portales Market.

Mercado de la Merced—a fifteen-minute walk from the Zócalo, the central main square of Mexico City—is a monumental temple to human appetite that has stood in various incarnations for centuries. Since the Spanish conquest in the sixteenth century, La Merced, as it is commonly known, has been the city's place to procure ingredients from anywhere in the country; at one time, it was thought to be the world's largest food market.

The designation La Merced refers both to a physical market (an echoing, massive structure built in the 1960s) and to the informal outdoor bazaars that surround it for a span of at least fifty-three city blocks, where the air is filled with the scents of mesquite grilling and cooked maize and the cries of food vendors. It is truly a feast for the senses.

"Jitomates, a-quince a-quince a-quince!" (Tomatoes, fifteen pesos a kilo!) Potatoes, onions, fresh chiles, squash! Zucchini blossoms, tamarind, jicama! Produce is hawked from stalls, tarpaulins on the ground, carts, and the backs of trucks by sellers calling their wares in a timeless ritual of enticement.

"Nopales, freshly picked this morning!" One of the indigenous women who travel from the countryside to sell traditional foods has tender young cactus paddles piled in stacks. Who wouldn't want to sit down to a zesty salad of fresh, clean-tasting cactus made aromatic with spearmint? So, seated on a folded blanket, the seller measures out a half kilo and deftly strips the thorns from them in moments flat.

It's a scene that calls to mind the legend of the city's founding: an Aztec priest, the story goes, spotted an eagle carrying a snake in its mouth perched on a nopal plant. The priest called on his people to come witness this promising portent, and as they watched, the cactus beneath the eagle grew into an island—eventually becoming Tenochtitlán, where the people would settle. Mystical significance aside, there are practical reasons to have settled in a region where nopal cactus grows: along with a vast assortment of other edible plants, it was an indicator of a bounteous food supply, as the volcanic soil in and around Mexico City—along with the year-round moderate temperature, sufficient rainfall, and sources of underground water—contributes to a region of remarkable fertility.

Inside La Merced, in one of its roughly five thousand stalls, a man unties a stack of dried corn husks; these will be used to wrap tamales, masa cakes that are stuffed with filling before being swaddled in corn husks or banana leaves and then steamed. Corn husk is but one item the market has an entire district dedicated to. The area where dried chiles are sold has seemingly infinite varieties of chiles stacked a yard high. The range of avocados is equally staggering, especially for someone who is familiar with the only one or two types found in supermarkets north of the border.

The fruit section is a kaleidoscope of color and fragrance. *Diableros*, carriers for hire, weave in and out of the throng, maneuvering groaning loads of plantains, fresh herbs, and sugarcane.

O utside, the sun is climbing as the afternoon peaks. Carefully, so as not to spill a drop, a little boy is attempting to carry several glasses of pale yellow *agua de guayaba*, a cooling guava drink, to his family's pickup truck; his big sister rushes to help. From the bed of the truck, their parents are selling tomatillos piled high in baskets, along with bundles of oregano, basil, thyme, epazote, and *verdolagas*, or purslane, a wild succulent with an appealing sour flavor. The tomatillos, which resemble small green tomatoes nestled in leafy husks, have a dense flesh and an assertive tartness that shines in everything from braised meat dishes to salsa verde. This family is selling two of the main ingredients for *pollo con verdolagas*, a spicy, saucy chicken and purslane stew with tomatillo salsa. After a long afternoon of shopping, it would be a perfect meal, especially paired with a stack of hot tortillas to soak up the sauce, and a cold beer.

As the shadows lengthen, though, the idea of going home to cook may well take a back seat to a burgeoning hunger. Happily, at one of the countless food stalls, a vendor is serving *calabazas a la mexicana*, zucchini stewed with poblano chiles. The foodways of Mexico City may be irrepressibly bold, but beneath the surface there is nuance. This dish, for instance, which could be characterized as Mexico's ratatouille, has a delicate herbaceous nature. The cook, a genial woman in a lavender apron, is happy to share the recipe.

"It's very simple," she says. "You sauté garlic and onion, add the poblano and cook it until it has wilted, and then comes the tomato and zucchini. You stew this covered until the zucchini is tender. I use bay leaves, too." On its surface, it indeed seems simple. But how does she achieve such tantalizing flavor and sweetness and savor? "Oh, you know how it is," she says. "In Mexico, we have a way with vegetables."

Victoria Colin de Orube
with her eight-year-old
granddaughter, Valentina,
holding Ancho Chiles
Stuffed with Manchego
Cheese (page 89).

Green Gold

To meet Jorge Corsica, a local chef who lives on the southernmost outskirts of Mexico City, we went on a long journey, traversing the foothills of the Teutli volcano. Milpa Alta, the proper name for this largely rural *delegación*, is agricultural, producing 90 percent of the nopal cactus consumed in the rest of greater Mexico City. "Green gold," Corsica calls it. He is not alone in seeing it as precious; the nopal plant is featured on Mexico's coat of arms. In addition to being nutritious and easy to cook, the cactus is home to the cochineal, an insect used for millennia for valuable pigment. Aztec legend has it that two gods fought so violently for possession of the nopal that drops of their blood fell on the cochineal, producing its bright red color.

Out in the nopal field, with its sweeping view, the mountain mist caresses our faces. Baskets in hand, we go in search of the biggest, most mature plants, which paradoxically bear the youngest paddles: some are the size of a pinkie fingernail and can be eaten raw, immature spines and all. Those that we will harvest are slightly bigger but still far more crisp and tangy than those at the markets. We pick them cautiously, careful not to split them.

Corsica strips our bounty of thorns and places the paddles directly on the hot comal. Ten minutes later I tuck one into a warm blue-corn tortilla with panela (a mozzarella-like cheese), a slice of avocado, and fresh salsa. The bright flavors are enhanced by the crisp mountain air. —*Margot Castañeda, gastronomy editor of* Chilango *magazine and former editor-in-chief of the Spanish version of Vice's* Munchies

Jorge Corsica harvests nopales in Milpa Alta, located in the southern part of the city. The nopales are then quick-roasted on a comal for breakfast.

*Above: Cactus and Mint
Salad (page 90). Opposite: a
field of nopales in Milpa Alta.*

"Mexican food is about the people who prepare it, eat it, and enjoy it. It's made from secrets, from recipes transmitted from generation to generation, our contradictions and our flavors. It is a reunion, it is satisfaction. It is an integration of its history, of the influences brought by commerce and by the conquests that have left, each time, wisdom that has continued to enrich the cuisine and the creativity of the people who make it."

—MÓNICA PATIÑO, CHEF-OWNER OF CASA VIRGINIA

Ancho Chiles Stuffed with Manchego Cheese

Chiles Anchos Rellenos

Chiles rellenos—chiles stuffed with cheese, coated with a beaten-until-stiff egg batter, fried, then served bathed in a tomato sauce—are typically made with poblano chiles whose skin has been charred. This easier-to-make alternative calls for ancho chiles, or dried poblanos, with a savory taste that's meaty, sweet, and satisfying in a way that only a softened dry chile is. When home cook Victoria Colín de Orube makes this dish for a gathering, she keeps the cooked chiles separate from the tomato sauce until company arrives, then ladles the sauce over each portion upon serving. These are typically eaten with a side dish of Mexican-Style Stewed Beans (page 192) and hot tortillas.

Serves 5

- 5 ancho chiles, stems intact
- About 10 ounces good melting cheese (such as Manchego, Chihuahua, ranchero, or panela, or a combination; see Cheeses, page 193), very thinly sliced
- ⅓ cup all-purpose flour
- 2 egg whites
- 1 egg yolk
- About 1½ cups canola oil, for frying
- About 3½ cups Mexican Tomato Sauce (page 201), heated

1 Clip off the top of the stem of each chile, leaving only ¼ inch intact. Using a paring knife, cut a lengthwise slit in each chile, leaving about ½ inch uncut at the stem end and at the bottom. Remove the seeds and membranes and discard, then rinse the chiles under cold running water. Fill a medium saucepan with water and bring it to a rolling boil. Turn off the heat, fully submerge the chiles in the water, and let soak until they have just turned soft, about 5 minutes. Drain them, pat them dry inside and out with paper towels, and set aside.

2 Stuff each chile with five or six slices (about 2 ounces) of the cheese. Tuck one side of the chile skin inside the other, forming a loose seal. Put the flour onto a flat dinner plate or other flat surface and level it with your fingers. One at a time, lightly dredge the stuffed chiles in the flour, coating evenly and tapping off the excess, and set aside on a large plate.

3 Put the egg whites into a medium bowl. Using a handheld mixer or a whisk, beat the egg whites until dry, stiff peaks form. Add the egg yolk and continue beating until the yolk is fully incorporated and soft peaks form.

4 Line a large plate with paper towels. Pour the oil to a depth of 1 inch into a medium skillet and heat over medium heat. To test if the oil is ready, drop in a smidgen of the egg mixture; if bubbles form around it instantly, the oil is ready.

5 Gently place a chile into the beaten eggs and carefully roll it, using your hands or two spoons, until all sides are coated in a layer of the egg mixture about ¼ inch thick. Make sure the entire surface of the chile is covered.

6 Using two spoons, add the coated chile to the hot oil. If the chile is not fully covered in beaten egg, you can add a spoonful or two more at this point. Fry one side, spooning hot oil over the top to hasten cooking, until the bottom starts to turn golden, about 1½ minutes. Turn the chile and fry on the other side until it begins turning golden, about 1 minute. As the chile cooks, make sure its entire surface comes in contact with the hot oil, turning the chile and tilting the pan as needed. When the chile is golden on all sides, transfer it to the towel-lined plate. Repeat with remaining stuffed chiles, coating them first with the flour and then the eggs and then frying them until golden.

Chicken and Purslane Stew with Tomatillo Salsa (page 91).

7 Place each fried chile on an individual plate. Ladle a generous ¾ cup of the tomato sauce over each chile and serve right away.

Mexican-Style Stewed Zucchini and Poblanos
Calabazas a la Mexicana

This simple, easy-to-make, and satisfying vegetarian dish (see photographs, pages ii and 77) is a sort of Mexican ratatouille seasoned with oregano. It's a style of vegetable preparation that is widespread in Mexico and is typically served as a side dish. It makes a marvelous main course, however, especially when topped with a lashing of *crema*, Mexico's sour cream (see page 197), and a good sprinkling of Cotija cheese to make it extra rich. If squash blossoms are available, add a couple of handfuls of them whole with the zucchini. You can also substitute whole green beans for the zucchini with equally good results.

Serves 4

> 3 tablespoons canola oil
> 1 medium white onion, cut into ¼-inch dice
> 2 garlic cloves, coarsely chopped
> 2 poblano chiles, stemmed, seeded, and cut into 1½-inch squares
> 3 medium Roma tomatoes, coarsely chopped
> 7 small zucchini, cut into 1½-inch cubes
> Salt
> ½ teaspoon oregano

1 Heat a medium saucepan over medium heat. When the pan is hot, add the oil. When the oil is hot, add the onion and cook, stirring constantly, just until it begins to turn translucent, about 3 minutes. Add the garlic and continue to cook, stirring constantly, until the garlic begins to soften, about 2 minutes. Add the chiles and continue to cook, stirring often, until the chiles begin to wilt, about 7 minutes. Add the tomatoes, zucchini, 1 teaspoon salt, and the oregano and stir well. Cover and continue to cook at a lively simmer until the zucchini is tender but still slightly al dente in the center, 25 to 30 minutes.

2 Taste for salt and add more if needed. Transfer to a platter and serve right away.

Cactus and Mint Salad
Ensalada de Nopales

Nopales, or cactus paddles (see photograph, page 82), which grow in Mexico and in the southwestern United States, are usually available wherever there are Mexican grocers. Only the fresh ones will do for this recipe; nopales sold in jars do not have the same flavor or texture. This salad (see photograph, page 84) sparkles with clean, fresh flavors and works well in almost any context. It is equally good whether as a table condiment, a side dish, an appetizer, or eaten straight out of the bowl with warm tortillas. It makes for a tangy, zesty garnish for the fava bean–stuffed tlacoyos on page 68, and if you embellish it with a handful of crumbled aged Mexican cheese, sliced radishes, and a coarse-chopped avocado, it can even be a main course.

Serves 4

> Salt
> 8 medium nopales (see page 202), thorns removed and cut into strips about 1½ inches long by ¼ inch wide (about 4 cups)
> 1 cup finely chopped Roma tomatoes
> ½ small white onion, finely chopped
> ½ cup firmly packed fresh spearmint or peppermint leaves, finely chopped
> 2 tablespoons freshly squeezed lime juice
> 2 tablespoons extra-virgin olive oil

1 Bring a medium saucepan filled with water to a boil and add 1 teaspoon salt. Drop the nopales into the boiling water and cook until their bright green raw color turns a drab olive hue and they are tender, about 5 minutes. Drain them in a colander and rinse thoroughly with cold running water, gently massaging them with your hands. The goal is to rid them of as much of their clear, slimy juice as possible, which may take a couple of minutes. Drain well.

2 Transfer the nopales to a serving bowl and add the tomatoes, onion, and mint. Stir gently to combine, then add the lime juice, oil, and ½ teaspoon salt. Taste and add more salt if needed.

3 Let the salad sit at room temperature for at least 15 minutes before serving. It will keep covered in the refrigerator for up to a few days. Bring to room temperature before serving.

Chicken and Purslane Stew with Tomatillo Salsa

Pollo con Verdolagas

Although purslane, a tart succulent, grows wild in many parts of North America, this dish (see photograph, page 88) of chicken cooked in a spicy tomatillo sauce with purslane is nearly impossible to find served outside of Mexico. Soupy and sour with a kick from serrano chiles, it calls for plenty of tortillas for mopping up the highly seasoned sauce.

Serves 4

2¼ pounds bone-in, skin-on chicken
    drumsticks and thighs
1 medium white onion, halved
6 garlic cloves
2 bay leaves
5 whole allspice berries
Salt
4 cilantro sprigs
7 medium tomatillos, husks removed, rinsed,
    and quartered (about 3½ cups)
2 to 4 serrano chiles, stemmed and
    coarsely chopped
3 tablespoons canola oil
8 cups purslane leaves (see page 202),
    stems included, in 3-inch pieces

1 In a large pot, combine the chicken, half of the onion, two of the garlic cloves, the bay leaves, allspice, and 1 teaspoon salt. Add water to cover by about 1 inch, stir well, and bring to a boil over high heat. Turn down the heat to medium; you want to maintain a steady simmer

throughout the cooking process. Cook the chicken, stirring occasionally and skimming off any foam that forms, until cooked through, 30 to 35 minutes. Reserve 1 cup of the broth and set aside.

2 Meanwhile, begin making the sauce. In a blender, combine the cilantro, tomatillos, chiles (if you prefer a milder dish, use only two chiles), the remaining onion half and four garlic cloves, ½ teaspoon salt, and the reserved broth, and blend to a semismooth liquid.

3 Heat a Dutch oven or other large, heavy pot over medium heat. When the pot is hot, add the oil. When the oil is shimmering, add the tomatillo sauce (be careful, as it will splatter), stir immediately, and turn down the heat to low. Cook at a lively simmer, stirring often, until it darkens a bit and no longer tastes raw, about 10 minutes.

4 Using tongs or a slotted spoon, transfer the chicken pieces to the sauce (strain the remaining broth and reserve for another use), then add the purslane. Cook, stirring occasionally, until the purslane is fully wilted, 10 to 15 minutes. Avoid overcooking the purslane; it shouldn't be extremely mushy. Taste for salt and add more if needed.

5 Remove from the heat and let rest for about 10 minutes before serving to allow the flavors to marry.

5

Passion as Deep as the Sea

Seafood

This photo: Mexican Paella with Seafood, Chicken, and Pork Ribs (page 108) is a specialty at Cocina Mi Fonda restaurant. Page 92: Contramar's beloved Tuna and Avocado Tostadas (page 108).

Dark red guajillo chiles give this braised octopus (page 110) its earthy color.

Stroll along the tree-lined Calle de Durango in Colonia Roma Norte at about noon and you'll come upon a throng of people packing into Contramar, a pin on the map of any serious gastronome. The restaurant's world-class food and casual elegance draw people holding passports from every nation, and it's mainly the foreigners, accustomed to an early lunch, who constitute this first wave of diners. Many have come to relish the tuna tostada that they've heard so much about, and rightly so. A reinterpretation of classic ceviche, the dish is a mini tostada topped with tuna fillet marinated in orange juice and soy sauce and garnished with chipotle mayonnaise, avocado, and a distinctly modern frizzle of flash-fried leeks. Biting into its fresh-tasting, balanced flavors and textures brings home the intelligence and directness of the Mexican approach to seafood.

Lunch, or *comida*, is the meal Mexico City dines out for, customarily at three o'clock. Thus no sooner has Contramar's wait staff changed the table linens than the dining room is flooded with a second wave of patrons, locals this time, eager for dishes like octopus cocktail, which they know will be of the highest quality. Mexicans are fond of seafood that is served raw or, in some cases (shrimp, for instance), briefly poached. Such dishes, from oysters on the half-shell to ceviche, are typically seasoned with fresh

lime juice, finely chopped onions and cilantro, and avocado scooped directly from the shell. A few shakes of Valentina hot sauce and sometimes Worcestershire complete the dish; this approach parallels the treatment Mexico City residents give to *michelada*, or spiked beer. While one might assume that adding such a profusion of ingredients would overwhelm the taste of the seafood, it is in fact a way to showcase and support the pure ocean flavors. Of course, cooked dishes, like spicy, tomatoey pasta con camarones, are also cherished.

Contramar is the brainchild of chef and owner Gabriela Cámara, who has a sparkling sense of humor and a flair for the dramatic. She is also an excellent businessperson. In 2015 Cámara looked to Mexico's northern neighbor and opened Cala in San Francisco, which became as renowned for its social-justice hiring practices as for its haute-cuisine Mexican food. Contramar, the place that started it all, was born of Cámara's desire to re-create her childhood memories of family trips to Acapulco. That seaport is home to famed seafood restaurants where vacationers go to drink beer, peel shrimp, and be serenaded by mariachis. Cámara's establishment captures the relaxed revelry of that experience and refines it. "The restaurant is a love letter," she says.

Cámara is not the only native with a strong connection to eating seafood. In fact, despite being geographically removed from both coasts

and located at an altitude of over seven thousand feet, the city's people have had a passion for seafood ever since the city was known as Tenochtitlán. Archaeological digs have unearthed ancient tombs and crypts that house collections of fish and seashells, testifying to what appears to be a rather mystical affinity for the fruits of the sea—mystical, considering that the terrain that must be traversed to get from coastline to city is rugged even now, and would have been treacherous before the advent of paved roads. Given that seafood is just about the most perishable foodstuff there is, and modern refrigeration was invented a scant century ago, the fortitude demonstrated by those early epicures is awe-inspiring.

Today, the landlocked metropolis consumes more seafood per capita than almost anywhere else on earth. And because of its geographical access to both the cold water of the Atlantic and the warm Pacific currents, few places can match it for sheer variety: after Tokyo's Tosoyu, formerly Tsukjii, Mexico City's La Nueva Viga is the largest seafood market in the world.

The first edition of La Nueva Viga was established in the nineteenth century near La Viga Canal, which linked the nearby cities of Xochimilco and Chalco geographically to the historical center of the city. A hundred years later, the canal was drained, paved over as a roadway, and named Calzada de la Viga, around which neighborhoods formed. The old building still stands, but a newer, behemoth version was built in the 1990s, when the demand for wholesale seafood outpaced the old market's capacity for distribution. Its newer incarnation is one of the most important markets in Latin America: order seafood at any Mexico City eatery, from spicy braised shrimp at Cantina la Reforma to crab rolls at Contramar, and it will have been sourced from La Nueva Viga.

Fishmongers in neighborhood markets see plenty of customers as well. The residents of Mexico City may be some distance from the coast, but home cooks typically have more than a few seafood recipes in their repertoire, whether they excel at cooking a straightforward but irresistible dish like *pulpo al guajillo*, dry-braised octopus flavored with garlic and chiles, or bring out a showstopper like *paella mexicana*, which features chicken, shrimp, and clams cooked in rice seasoned with saffron and paprika.

Inland Ocean

I never imagined that I would end up in the seafood business. Although others in my family have been working for La Nueva Viga since my uncle started there more than fifty years ago, I used to work in a department store; every morning I went to work in a suit and tie. One day my mother, who at the time was in charge of the warehouse at La Nueva Viga, asked me, "Why don't you come work here during your vacation?" I still don't know exactly what it was that caught my fancy—waking at dawn, the smell of the fish, the bustle of the market—but it captivated me. I quit my job at the department store and never looked back. When I'm here, I feel that I am part of something much larger. Fishermen from all over Mexico—people who work in both the Pacific and Atlantic—strive to make seafood arrive at the market at the utmost freshness. My clients, who used to be primarily street vendors, small restaurants, and housewives, are now supermarkets and larger restaurants. We had to invest to improve and keep up with the demand; I even went to get a degree in business administration. This is a noble job. It supports my family and many workers and offers healthy and nutritious food for the Mexican people. *—Abel Hernández, manager of El Ostioncito, a wholesale oyster shop in La Nueva Viga*

At La Nueva Viga Market, fresh seafood, such as this sea bass sliced into steaks, is purchased mainly for resale in supermarkets and restaurants.

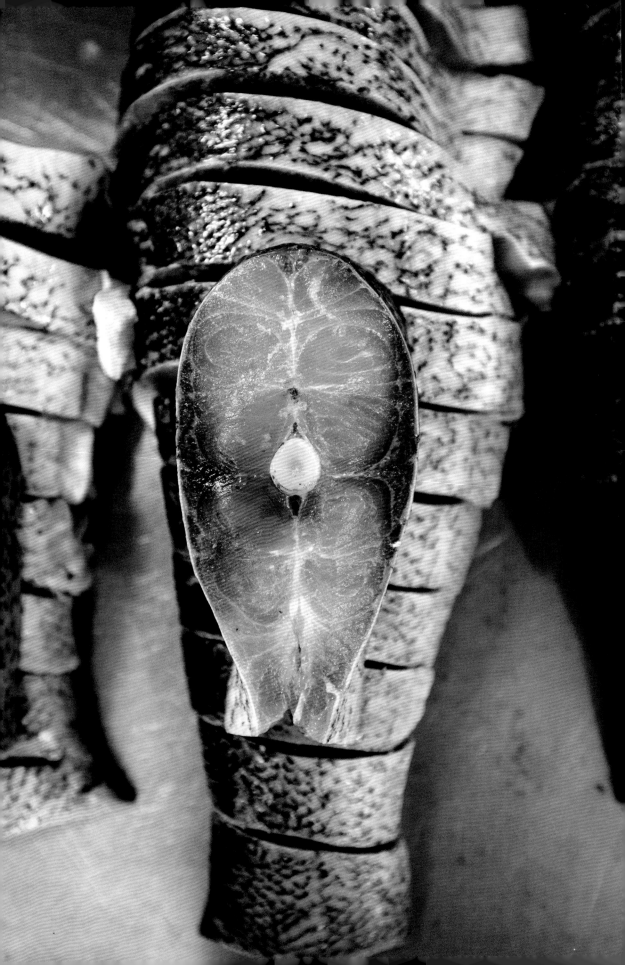

"When we opened Contramar in 1998, we emphasized local ingredients. At the time it was considered a great risk to limit yourself like that. Now everyone is eager for Mexican food. Our country has a history of ingredient exchange thanks to the confluence of different cultures that are found here. But I think Mexico has always been at the center of the culinary world."

—GABRIELA CÁMARA, CHEF-OWNER OF CONTRAMAR RESTAURANT

At Boca del Rio restaurant,
seafood cocktail (page 112) is
served with cilantro, chopped
onion, and avocado.

Feliz Navidad

When Mexicans say "Navidad," we mean Christmas Eve. "What will you do on the twenty-fourth?" we ask one another, as if we didn't already know the answer: dine with those we love. In our family, my mother cooks Grandma Paulina's *bacalao*, salt cod stew; my dad (the man at right, serving pasta) prepares Grandma Haydée's shrimp broth, and my sister, Arlette, assembles *ensalada de manzana*, the traditional Christmas salad made with apples, jicama, and beets—and which, among all of us, only she and Mom really enjoy. Beets are a highly contentious ingredient in our family! I take pleasure in wondering what wonderful new dishes will supplant my generation's.

December 25 is the Día del Recalentado, or "Leftovers Day," when everything tastes even better. This day is like a séance, for the flavors link me to the past. The reheated roast turkey returns me to my grandparents' house and to playing with my cousins; the Christmas punch calls forth the confusion and laughter of when Arlette and I were teenagers; the leftover bacalao invokes one more spring our family will spend together, since we freeze an extra portion to eat then. For now, though, chocolate cake is served, our ritual dessert. This is our time of remembrances. —*Gabriela Damián Miravete, a Mexico City–based essayist and sci-fi writer*

Contramar-Style Tuna and Avocado Tostadas

Tostadas de Atún de Contramar

This recipe (see photograph, page 92) is based on one of the signature appetizers at the Mexico City restaurant Contramar: fresh tuna marinated in orange juice and soy sauce, embellished with chipotle mayonnaise and flash-fried leeks, atop a tostada.

Makes 8 tostadas

½ cup canola oil

7-inch piece leek, white part only, cleaned and cut into ¼-inch-thick slices and separated into individual rings

5 tablespoons mayonnaise

4 teaspoons sauce from canned chipotle chiles (see page 195)

Juice of 1 orange

4 teaspoons soy sauce

1 teaspoon freshly squeezed lime juice

Salt

7 ounces sushi-grade tuna belly fillet, cut into thin 2 by 1-inch slices (about 24 slices)

Eight 6-inch tostadas (page 202)

1 ripe medium avocado, halved, pitted, peeled, and cut lengthwise into ¼-inch-thick slices

3 limes, quartered, for serving

1 Line a plate with paper towels. In a medium saucepan, heat the oil over medium heat. When the oil is hot, working in batches, add the leek slices and fry until just golden and slightly crisp, about 2 minutes. Set aside on the plate.

2 In a bowl, stir together the mayonnaise and canned chipotle sauce; set aside. In another bowl, stir together the orange juice, soy sauce, and lime juice. Taste for salt, adding some if needed. Add the tuna and marinate for 10 minutes, then discard the marinade.

3 Spread about 2 teaspoons of the chipotle mayonnaise on each tostada. Lay about three tuna slices on top of each tostada as shown in the photograph on page 92, followed by about 1 tablespoon fried leek and two or three avocado slices. Serve at once, accompanied by the limes for squeezing on top.

Mexican Paella with Seafood, Chicken, and Pork Ribs

Paella Mexicana

Bustling Calle López is home to Cocina Mi Fonda, a homey restaurant where the aroma of paella (see photograph, page 94) billows tantalizingly out onto the street. This recipe, based on one of theirs, is a real people-pleaser—and doesn't require a paella pan.

Serves 6

4 cups Mexican Chicken Broth (page 194)

1 teaspoon saffron threads

4 tablespoons extra-virgin olive oil

2 bone-in, skin-on chicken thighs, each cut in half

2 bone-in, skin-on chicken drumsticks

8 ounces baby-back pork ribs (about 4 ribs), separated into individual ribs and halved crosswise if possible

1 medium white onion, minced

3 garlic cloves, minced

3 medium Roma tomatoes, chopped

2 teaspoons sweet paprika

Salt

1 green bell pepper, seeded and cut into 1½-inch-wide chunks

2 cups parboiled rice (see page 199)

12 cherrystone or other medium clams (about 1¾ pounds)

12 medium head-on shrimp in the shell (about ¾ pound)

Grilled Tomato and Green Chile Salsa (page 200), for serving

1 In a medium saucepan, bring the broth to a boil. Add the saffron, turn down the heat, and simmer until the liquid is a deep gold,

Boca del Rio–Style Oysters (page 113).

about 5 minutes. Remove from the heat, strain through a fine-mesh sieve into a heatproof bowl, and set aside.

2 In a 5-quart pot with sides no more than 4 inches high, heat 2 tablespoons of the oil over medium heat. When the oil is hot, and working in batches to prevent overcrowding, add the chicken and pork and cook, turning often, until golden on all sides, 7 to 10 minutes. Transfer to a plate. Turn down the heat to medium-low and add the remaining 2 tablespoons oil and the onion. Stir often throughout the following process: Cook the onion until translucent, about 5 minutes. Add the garlic and cook until it starts softening, about 3 minutes. Add the tomatoes, paprika, and 1½ teaspoons salt and cook until the tomatoes have softened somewhat, about 6 minutes.

3 Return the chicken and pork to the pan, add the green pepper and reserved broth, and turn up the heat to high. When the liquid begins to boil, turn down the heat and simmer just until the meat is no longer raw at the center, about 15 minutes. Check the chicken and pork at their thickest points to confirm. Taste for salt and adjust if needed.

4 Sprinkle the rice evenly into the liquid, making sure it is mostly submerged. Arrange the clams on the surface of the rice, then turn up the heat to high. When the liquid starts to boil, turn down the heat to low, cover, and cook undisturbed for 7 minutes. Remove the lid and cook undisturbed for 15 minutes longer. Stir the shrimp into the rice and cook until all of the liquid has evaporated, the rice is cooked through, and the shrimp is fully cooked, 15 to 20 minutes longer.

5 Remove from the heat and let rest for 5 to 10 minutes; discard clams that haven't opened. Serve the paella with the salsa alongside.

Braised Octopus with Garlic and Guajillo Chiles
Pulpo al Guajillo

Even diners unadventurous about seafood tend to be won over by this braise of tender octopus spiced with guajillo chile and garlic (see photograph, page 97). This recipe is based on one from home cook Verónica Sánchez Félix, whose family loves to eat it with hot tortillas, fresh salsa, and sliced avocado.

Serves 6

  1 fresh or frozen whole octopus, 3 to 4 pounds
  ½ medium white onion
  15 garlic cloves, 2 whole and 13 thinly sliced
  Salt
  8 guajillo chiles, stemmed, seeded, and cut crosswise into ¼-inch pieces
  ¼ cup extra-virgin olive oil
  2 or 3 limes, quartered, for serving

1 If using a whole fresh octopus, ask your fishmonger to clean it for you; to do it yourself, see the instructions on page 199. If using a frozen octopus, let it thaw overnight in the refrigerator. Rinse the octopus under cold running water. Put it into a large, heavy pot and add the onion, whole garlic cloves, 1 teaspoon salt, and water to cover by 2 inches. Bring to a rolling boil, then immediately turn down the heat, cover partially, and simmer until the octopus is tender enough to be easily pierced with a fork, 1 to 1½ hours. Lift the octopus out of the pot, draining it well, and set aside on a cutting board. Reserve 1½ cups of the broth. Discard the remaining broth.

2 While the octopus is cooling, submerge the sliced chiles in a bowl of hot water until softened, about 10 minutes. Drain the chiles and set aside. When the octopus is cool enough to handle, cut the entire octopus into bite-size pieces about ½ inch in diameter.

Salt Cod Stew with Potatoes and Olives (page 113).

3 Heat a 12-inch skillet over medium-low heat. When the pan is hot, add the oil. When the oil is hot, add the thinly sliced garlic and the softened chiles and cook, stirring constantly, until the garlic has softened considerably, about 5 minutes. Add the reserved broth, stir, turn up the heat slightly, and simmer at a lively bubble until the liquid is reduced by about half, about 10 minutes. Add the octopus and cook, stirring occasionally, until it has taken on the flavor of the sauce and nearly all of the liquid has evaporated, 15 to 20 minutes longer. Taste for salt, adding more if needed. Serve with the limes for squeezing on top.

Cantina-Style Shrimp with Carrots, Chiles, Olives, and Potatoes

Camarones a la Vizcaína

There's nothing quite like sitting down to a boldly seasoned, restorative dish like this one along with a glass of cold beer or a shot of mezcal. A maximalist braise of shrimp, potatoes, carrots, olives, and pickled chiles, this heady and traditional combination (see photograph, page 98) is typically eaten with crusty bread—as it is at Cantina la Reforma, whose rendition inspired this recipe.

Serves 5

3 tablespoons extra-virgin olive oil

½ medium white onion, minced

3 garlic cloves, minced

5 bay leaves

3 thyme sprigs, or ½ teaspoon dried thyme

½ cup green olives (such as Manzanilla or Picholine), with pits

7 chiles güeros encurtidos (see page 195) plus 1 tablespoon of their juice and some of the carrots in the jar, if any, or pepperoncini

3 medium Roma tomatoes, minced

1 medium carrot, peeled and cut into ⅓-inch cubes

1 medium white waxy potato, peeled and cut into ⅓-inch cubes

1 pound medium to large head-on shrimp in the shell, antennae removed

Freshly ground black pepper

Salt

Crusty bread, for serving

1 Heat a 12-inch skillet over medium heat. When the pan is hot, add the oil. When the oil is hot, add the onion, then stir often throughout the following process: Cook the onion until translucent, about 5 minutes. Add the garlic, bay leaves, and thyme and cook until the garlic and onion are just starting to become golden, about 5 minutes. Add the olives and the chiles and their juice and cook for 4 minutes. Add the tomatoes, carrots, and potatoes, cover, and cook, stirring often, until the carrots and potatoes are fork-tender, 10 to 15 minutes.

2 Add the shrimp and a few grinds of black pepper and cook, covered but stirring often, until the shrimp are cooked through, 10 to 15 minutes; the timing will depend on their size.

3 Salt to taste, then transfer to a serving dish. Serve at once with the bread.

Mexican-Style Shrimp Cocktail

Coctel de Camarones

The seasonings used here, which form the foundation of the Mexican-style seafood cocktail, strike the perfect balance of tart, sweet, and spicy. The recipe calls for cooking the shrimp, but raw bay scallops (see photograph, page 104) or oysters are just as commonly used. Serve with plenty of saltine crackers.

Serves 4

1½ medium white onions, whole onion finely chopped and onion half left whole

2 garlic cloves

2½ pounds medium shrimp in the shell

1 cup ketchup

1 cup Clamato

¼ cup freshly squeezed lime juice

½ cup loosely packed fresh cilantro leaves, minced

1 ripe small avocado, quartered

2 limes, halved

Worcestershire sauce, for serving

Bottled Mexican hot sauce (such as Valentina or Tapatío), for serving

Saltine crackers, for serving

1 In a medium saucepan, combine the onion half and garlic, add a few inches of water, and bring to a boil. Add the shrimp and boil until cooked through, 3 to 6 minutes. Drain into a colander, discard the onion and garlic, and rinse the shrimp under cold running water until cool. Peel the shrimp, discarding the heads if attached. Refrigerate in a covered container until ready to serve.

2 In a medium bowl, stir together the ketchup, Clamato, and lime juice. Add the chopped onion, shrimp, and cilantro and mix.

3 Spoon the shrimp mixture into four individual serving glasses and top each serving with one-fourth of the avocado. Serve at once with the limes, Worcestershire, and hot sauce for adding to taste, with the crackers on the side.

Boca del Rio–Style Oysters

Ostiones en Su Concha

This recipe (see photograph, page 109), based on one from the 1950s-style Boca del Rio restaurant in the San Cosme neighborhood, is a simple and exuberantly flavored deconstructed seafood cocktail: oysters on the half shell complemented with chopped onion, cilantro, and avocado, plus a splash each of Worcestershire, hot sauce, and lime juice—an irresistible combination.

Serves 1

6 oysters in the shell

2 tablespoons minced white onion

1 tablespoon minced fresh cilantro

¼ ripe medium avocado, sliced

Worcestershire sauce, for topping

Bottled Mexican hot sauce (such as Valentina or Tapatío), for topping

½ lime, for squeezing on top

Saltine crackers, for serving

Shuck the oysters and arrange them on their half-shells on a serving plate. Top each oyster first with the onion, then the cilantro, then about ½ slice or so of the avocado. Add a shake of Worcestershire and hot sauce plus a squeeze of lime juice to each, and serve at once with the crackers.

Salt Cod Stew with Potatoes and Olives

Bacalao a la Vizcaína

This Spanish-inspired stew of *bacalao* (salt cod) braised with new potatoes, olives, and chiles (see photograph, page 111) is the centerpiece of nearly every Mexico City Christmas Eve dinner. The supporting ingredients, like the bacalao itself, are strongly flavored, so the best accompaniment is crusty bread or tortillas. The bacalao must be soaked the day before it is cooked, so plan ahead.

Serves 6

1 pound salt cod fillet

¼ cup skinless whole almonds

20 very small red new potatoes (1 to 1½ inches in diameter), peeled

Salt

½ cup extra-virgin olive oil

1 medium white onion, finely chopped

5 garlic cloves, finely chopped

¼ cup loosely packed fresh flat-leaf parsley leaves, minced

5 medium Roma tomatoes, finely chopped

2 tablespoons capers

½ cup green olives (such as Manzanilla or Picholine), with pits

6 chiles güeros encurtidos (see page 195) plus some of the carrots in the jar, if any, or pepperoncini

½ cup Mexican Chicken Broth (page 194), plus more if needed

Crusty bread, for serving

1 One day ahead of cooking, rehydrate the salt cod. Rinse it thoroughly, massaging it under cold running water. Put it in a large nonreactive bowl, add water to cover generously, cover, and refrigerate for 24 hours, changing the water at least four times and rinsing and massaging the cod each time. Drain it thoroughly. When you're ready to cook, shred it into the finest strips possible, carefully removing and discarding any errant bones or skin. Set the cod aside.

2 Fill a bowl with hot water, add the almonds, and soak for 1 hour. Drain well, chop finely, and set aside. In a medium saucepan, combine the potatoes with water to cover generously, bring to a boil, and boil until just fork tender, about 15 minutes. Drain and set aside.

3 In a large, heavy pot, heat the oil over medium heat. When the oil is hot, add the onion, then stir often throughout the following process: Cook the onion until translucent, about 4 minutes. Add the garlic and cook until it has softened, about 3 minutes. Add the parsley and cook for 2 minutes. Add the chopped almonds and cook for 2 minutes. Add the tomatoes and cook until they begin to break down, about 10 minutes. Add the cooked potatoes, shredded cod, capers, olives, chiles, and broth. Mix well and cook for 30 minutes. There should be just a little liquid remaining; add more broth if the pot begins to dry out. Serve accompanied with the bread.

Casa Virginia's Crab Tostadas

Tostadas de Jaiba de Casa Virginia

One bite of these crunchy tostadas topped with garlic-and-cilantro-scented crab (opposite), based on a favorite appetizer at Mónica Patiño's restaurant Casa Virginia, and you are transported to the seaside.

Makes 8 tostadas

> 3 tablespoons extra-virgin olive oil
> ½ medium white onion, half thickly sliced and half very finely chopped
> 1 garlic clove, bruised
> 12 ounces freshly cooked crabmeat (such as blue or Dungeness)
> Salt
> 1 serrano chile, stemmed, seeded, and minced
> 1 medium Roma tomato, minced
> ¾ cup loosely packed fresh cilantro leaves, minced
> 2 tablespoons freshly squeezed lime juice
> 1 teaspoon cider vinegar
> Eight 6-inch tostadas (page 202)
> ½ cup very finely shredded cabbage
> 1 ripe medium avocado, halved, pitted, peeled, and cut lengthwise into ¼-inch-thick slices
> 8 fresh fennel fronds, for garnish (optional)
> 2 to 3 limes, quartered, for serving

1 Heat a 12-inch skillet over medium-low heat. When the pan is hot, add 2 tablespoons of the oil, followed by the sliced onion and the garlic. Cook, stirring often, until golden, about 10 minutes. Discard the onion and garlic, leaving the seasoned oil in the pan. Add the crab and heat, stirring often, just until heated through and beginning to dry out, about 4 minutes. Taste the crab, adding salt if needed. Set the crab aside to cool.

2 In a bowl, combine the chopped onion, chile, tomato, cilantro, lime juice, vinegar, and the remaining 1 tablespoon oil and mix well. Add the crab and mix again.

3 Place about 2 heaping tablespoons of the crab mixture atop each tostada, using all of it. Top with about 1 tablespoon cabbage, followed by a slice or two of avocado and a fennel frond (if using). Serve at once, with the limes on the side.

Casa Virginia's seafood tostadas; the crab tostada (recipe above) is shown center.

6

Platos Fuertes, Pride on a Plate

Main Dishes

This photo: the pedestrian promenade in the center of Avenida Álvaro Obregón, in Mexico City's Roma Norte neighborhood. Page 116: Magali Alvarado Retana presents Milpa Alta Mole (page 138).

*Page 120: members of the
Orube Garcia family at their
Guadalajaran restaurant,
La Chiva Come. Page 121:
Carnitas Sandwiches with
Árbol Chile Sauce (page 139).*

I f a cook wants to master just one Mexican dish, they might consider a mole, which is not only one of Mexico's best main courses but also an unquestionably world-class dish.

Mole is an ornate creation, with a history dating back thousands of years. The word *mole* comes from the Nahuatl word *mulli*, meaning "sauce," and across Mexico, hundreds of variations are found. For example, in the state of Oaxaca alone, a day's drive from Mexico City, there are scores of versions, from a bright yellow kind that gets its color from zucchini blossoms to one that becomes pitch black with the addition of scorched chiles. But the version most widely known both inside and outside of Mexico is *mole poblano*, which originates from the city of Puebla, close to Mexico City.

The exact origins of *mole poblano* are contested and difficult to pin down, but its elaborate recipe, while not fixed, invariably incorporates European elements into the indigenous mole and is often composed of upward of thirty ingredients. These can run the gamut from dried fruits, such as prunes and raisins, and fresh fruit or vegetables (or both), like plantain or even pineapple, to seeds, nuts, and, of course, the inevitable amalgamation of chile varieties, with regional embellishments such as a touch of dark chocolate or crumbled sugar cookies.

Few cooks can claim to be as well versed in the preparation of a Puebla-style mole as those who reside in the rural community of San Pedro Atocpan, in Milpa Alta, Mexico City's southeast corner. It is a place not lacking in modern appurtenances, but it is still undeniably quaint: most of the houses were built before the turn of the last century, and burros tread alongside the cars that travel the cobblestone streets. Milpa Alta is known in part for its nopal fields (see photograph, page 85), but what truly distinguishes this particular place is that more than 90 percent of its population makes a living by producing mole. Their specialty is *mole almendrado*, for which nearly every family has its own closely guarded recipe.

Luis Juan Alvarado Retana, his wife, Martha, and their thirty-five-year-old daughter, Magali, are no exception. Like many of their neighbors, they have a small family-run enterprise producing the sauce professionally, and in a converted room set back in a courtyard, their tiny industrial kitchen is chugging away. In a charmingly analog process, the ingredients are toasted before making their way through a grating mechanism. From there, everything goes into the hopper and is ground into an earth-colored paste.

It is nearing the end of the workday and the courtyard is wreathed in aroma. Martha comes out of the factory kitchen wiping her hands on her apron. "It would be foolish," she points out wisely, "to visit San Pedro Atocpan without stopping to taste our mole!"

Mole is sometimes prepared without meat and poured over a dish like tamales, or even served atop a simple plate of rice. This afternoon, though, Magali has prepared poached chicken to eat with the family's mole. After the soup bowls of the first course have been cleared, Magali carries a steaming earthenware pot to the dining room. This is the *plato fuerte*, literally "strong plate," the most important dish in the Mexico City home, the showstopper for which a cook reserves their highest level of creativity.

Luis bestows a smile on his daughter, proud of her, and digs in. The sophistication of the mole's flavor is unmatched, as the individual ingredients have melded to create a compound of flavors that all reach the palate simultaneously.

Needless to say, mole almendrado is but one plato fuerte that might take pride of place on a table. What a Mexico City cook brings out with a flourish could just as easily be a roast dish, such *pierna de cordero con pasilla*, a honey-and-spice encrusted lamb served with oven-crisped pasilla chiles for crumbling on top. Roasts prepared in chile-based sauces are frequently featured as the centerpiece of lunch, with *lomo adobado* (see photograph, page 135), marinated pork loin cooked in a sauce made from beer, spices,

and three varieties of dried chile, among the choices. Another possibility is *carne en su jugo*, a homey Guadalajara-style beef-and-bean ragout that cries out for a hunk of crusty bread to sop up the juices. Or if a cook is really out to get a round of applause, they might serve *chiles en nogada*, in which poblano chiles are stuffed with spiced forcemeat and fruit, napped with a sauce that features goat cheese, sherry, and several types of ground nuts, and then finished with glistening pomegranate seeds. Of course, it could also be a mole—perhaps a green mole with chicken, chard, and parsley; or, in homage to San Pedro Atocpan, a velvety *mole almendrado*, with peanuts, almonds, cloves, and plantain. These dishes are not only delicious— they are a gateway to understanding how Mexican cooks combine unlikely ingredients to achieve breathtakingly complex flavor.

A vendor in Mercado de la
Merced; in the baskets are
garlic and habanero chiles of
varying degrees of ripeness.

"The Mexican kitchen is rooted in the ingredients our region provides us—and in knowing how to apply the right techniques to make those ingredients into delicious foods. For me, Mexican food is truly about knowing what to cook based on the season at hand."

—MÓNICA PATIÑO

Anchor of an Ancient Cuisine

Chiles are native to Mexico, and the varieties available there are truly staggering. From the tiny, intense piquín, one of Mexico's hottest, or the pasilla, which has a pleasingly bittersweet taste and is sometimes double the length of your hand, to the fresh árbol, a considerably smoldering forest-green specimen, the scope of their diversity is matched only by the range of use to which the Mexican cook puts them.

This abundance of chile varieties is one of the nation's great natural treasures, and not coincidentally, the chile is a cornerstone of Mexico City cuisine. The Mexican cook does not think of a chile solely in terms of its *picor* (spicy) aspects, what is thought of as Scoville units. Far more important is its flavor profile, for each chile has its own specific characteristics and uses.

If it is fresh, is it floral and super-spicy like the habanero? If it is sun-dried, does it have a meaty savor, like the chile ancho, or an earthier depth, like a chile negro? Some types can thicken a sauce nicely. Others are perfect for pickling or for grilling for salsa. For more information on buying and cooking with chiles, see page 195.

A stunning deep brick-red color, the **guajillo** *(opposite), the dried form of the mirasol chile, comes from Central Mexico. It ranges from mild to fiery hot, with a sweet, faintly bitter flavor.*

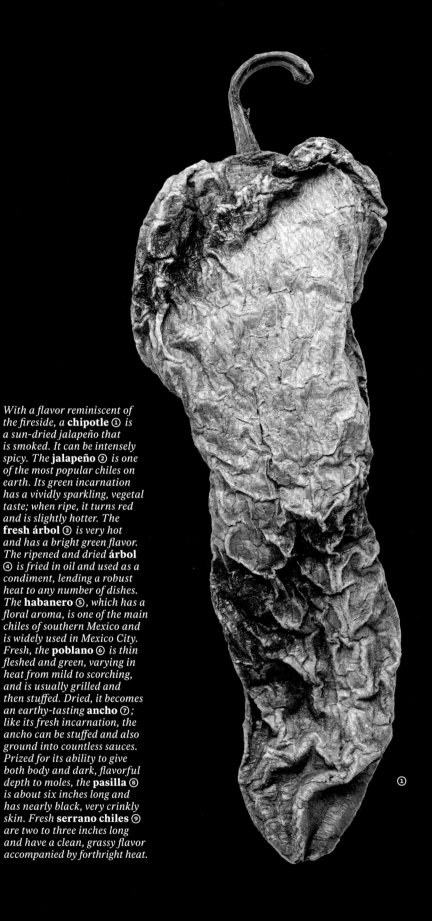

With a flavor reminiscent of
the fireside, a **chipotle** ① *is
a sun-dried jalapeño that
is smoked. It can be intensely
spicy. The* **jalapeño** ② *is one
of the most popular chiles on
earth. Its green incarnation
has a vividly sparkling, vegetal
taste; when ripe, it turns red
and is slightly hotter. The*
fresh árbol ③ *is very hot
and has a bright green flavor.
The ripened and dried* **árbol**
④ *is fried in oil and used as a
condiment, lending a robust
heat to any number of dishes.
The* **habanero** ⑤, *which has a
floral aroma, is one of the main
chiles of southern Mexico and
is widely used in Mexico City.
Fresh, the* **poblano** ⑥ *is thin
fleshed and green, varying in
heat from mild to scorching,
and is usually grilled and
then stuffed. Dried, it becomes
an earthy-tasting* **ancho** ⑦;
*like its fresh incarnation, the
ancho can be stuffed and also
ground into countless sauces.
Prized for its ability to give
both body and dark, flavorful
depth to moles, the* **pasilla** ⑧
*is about six inches long and
has nearly black, very crinkly
skin. Fresh* **serrano chiles** ⑨
*are two to three inches long
and have a clean, grassy flavor
accompanied by forthright heat.*

①

*Above: Green Mole
with Chicken (page 147).
Opposite: sunrise on
Calle Moneda.*

"When I was a child growing up in the countryside of Guanajuato state, my grandmother cooked enough food for a crowd—stews, roasts, handmade tortillas, you name it. She made everything with so much love. Nowadays, I'm a country girl living in the big city, but I strive to carry on the lessons she taught me. I'm so proud of my heritage."

—BEATRIZ DE LA ROSA, A HOME COOK LIVING IN CIUDAD SATÉLITE, A MEXICO CITY SUBURB

Beatriz de la Rosa holds
Pork Loin with Guajillo
Chile Sauce (page 141).

Pork Rib and Vegetable Stew with Ancho and Pasilla Chiles

Mole de Olla

A chile-infused stew of pork ribs, corn, carrots, chayote, green beans, and zucchini, this dish (see photograph, page xiv) is often made with beef (short ribs would be excellent), though pork is traditional. If possible, have your butcher cut the pork ribs in half crosswise.

Serves 6

2¼ pounds baby-back pork ribs, separated into individual ribs and halved crosswise

13 cups cold water

2 medium white onions, both halved; 1 onion half thickly sliced and 1 onion half minced

9 garlic cloves

Salt

2 ears corn, husked and cut crosswise into four pieces

4 epazote sprigs (see page 198), optional

2 cups hot water

1 tablespoon canola oil

4 ancho chiles, stemmed and seeded

4 pasilla chiles, stemmed and seeded

2 pinches of ground cumin

2 medium carrots, peeled, halved lengthwise, and cut crosswise into 3-inch chunks

1 medium chayote, peeled and cut lengthwise into pieces ½ inch thick (optional)

2 small white potatoes, peeled and cut into 3-inch chunks

25 green beans, stemmed and torn in half

4 small zucchini, cut lengthwise into 3-inch chunks

About 1 tablespoon dried oregano

4 limes, quartered, for serving

1 Put the pork into a stockpot, add the cold water, the whole onion halves, four of the garlic cloves, and 2 tablespoons salt, and stir to dissolve the salt. Bring the pot to a boil over high heat, turn down the heat to a steady simmer, and cook uncovered, stirring occasionally and skimming off any foam that forms on the surface, for 30 minutes. Add the corn and epazote (if using) and simmer, stirring occasionally and skimming as needed, until the meat is very tender, about 30 minutes longer.

2 Meanwhile, prepare the seasoning. Pour the hot water into a medium bowl. In a 12-inch skillet, heat the oil over medium heat. When the oil is hot, add all of the chiles and toast, turning once, until their surface softens slightly and they become fragrant, about 2 minutes. Transfer the chiles to the hot water and submerge, stirring them every so often, until they soften, about 10 minutes. Reserve the water.

3 While the oil is still hot, add the remaining five garlic cloves and the sliced onion half and cook, stirring constantly, just until they begin to pick up golden spots, about 4 minutes. Transfer the onion and garlic to a blender, add the softened chiles and their water and the cumin, and blend until very smooth.

4 Using a fine-mesh sieve, strain the blended chile mixture into the stockpot. Stir well; taste for salt, adding more if needed. Turn up the heat to medium-high and bring to a gentle rolling boil. Add the carrots, chayote (if using), potatoes, and green beans, turn down the heat, and simmer uncovered, stirring occasionally, until the vegetables are just fork-tender, about 30 minutes. Stir in the zucchini, cover partially, and cook, stirring occasionally, until the zucchini is very tender but not mushy, about 30 minutes. Taste again for salt, adding more as needed.

5 Remove the stew from the heat and let rest for 20 minutes. Garnish each serving with about 1 tablespoon minced onion and a generous pinch of oregano. Serve with the lime quarters for squeezing on top.

Stuffed Roasted Poblano Chiles with Walnut Sauce (page 142).

Milpa Alta Chicken Mole

Mole Almendrado de Don Luis

This luxurious sauce served with poached chicken (see photograph, page 116) is a close relative to the classic mole poblano that comes from the nearby city of Puebla. The recipe is inspired by the mole paste made in the small, family-run factory of Luis Juan Alvarado Retana in Milpa Alta.

Serves 6

- 3 bone-in, skin-on chicken thighs
- 3 bone-in, skin-on chicken drumsticks
- 14 whole allspice berries
- 4 cilantro sprigs
- 1 medium white onion, half left whole and half thickly sliced
- 4 garlic cloves
- Salt
- About 7 tablespoons canola oil, plus more if needed
- 5 pasilla chiles, stemmed and seeded
- 5 ancho chiles, stemmed and seeded
- 3 mulato chiles, stemmed and seeded
- 2 chipotle chiles, stemmed and seeded
- ½ cup blanched whole almonds
- 3 tablespoons sesame seeds
- 2 tablespoons roasted, skinless peanuts
- ½ teaspoon cumin seeds or ground cumin
- 5 whole cloves
- ½ teaspoon aniseeds
- 3 tablespoons raisins
- 1 very ripe small plantain (about 8 inches), peeled and cut into ½-inch-thick slices
- 1½ stale 6-inch corn tortillas
- 2 gingersnaps or butter cookies, broken into small pieces (about ¼ cup)
- ¼ teaspoon ground cinnamon
- ½ cup coarsely chopped Mexican chocolate (see page 169)

1 In a large pot, combine the chicken, four of the allspice berries, the cilantro, the whole onion half, two of the garlic cloves, and 2 teaspoons salt. Add water to cover by 1 to 2 inches and stir to dissolve the salt. Bring to a boil, turn down the heat to medium, and cook, maintaining a steady simmer, stirring occasionally and skimming off any foam that forms, until the chicken is cooked through, 30 to 35 minutes. Using tongs or a wire skimmer, transfer the chicken to a large plate and cover. Strain the broth through a fine-mesh sieve into a bowl and discard the solids; reserve the strained broth.

2 Meanwhile, fill a bowl with hot water. In a 12-inch skillet, heat 2 tablespoons of the oil over medium heat. Working in batches, add all of the chiles and toast, turning once, until their surface softens slightly and they become fragrant, about 2 minutes. Transfer the chiles to the hot water and soak until softened, about 10 minutes. Drain and set chiles aside.

3 While the oil is still hot (you may need to add a little more), add the remaining two garlic cloves and the remaining sliced onion and cook, stirring constantly, until they just begin to pick up golden spots, about 4 minutes. Set garlic and onion aside.

4 Return the skillet to low heat. When the pan is hot, add the almonds, sesame seeds, and peanuts and pan-roast, stirring often, until they begin to turn golden, about 5 minutes. Transfer to a plate. Return the pan to low heat, add the cumin, cloves, the remaining ten allspice berries, the aniseeds, and raisins and pan-roast, stirring often, until fragrant, about 2 minutes. Pour onto the plate with the almonds, sesame seeds, and peanuts.

5 Return the skillet to medium heat and add 2 tablespoons of the oil. When the oil is hot, add the plantain slices and fry, turning once, until golden, about 2 minutes on each side. Transfer the plantain slices to a plate, then add another 1 tablespoon oil to the skillet. When the oil is hot, add the tortillas and fry, turning once, until golden and slightly crispy, about 30 seconds per side. Remove from the heat; set tortillas aside.

6 In a food processor (or in batches in a blender), combine the chiles, garlic, and onion; the pan-roasted almonds, sesame seeds, peanuts, cumin, cloves, allspice, aniseeds, and raisins; the fried plantain and tortillas; the cookies and cinnamon; and 1 cup of the reserved broth. Grind the ingredients until they are very smooth; you may need to add another ½ cup broth to keep the mixture moving. Add 1½ teaspoons salt, stir well, taste, and add more salt if needed.

7 Heat a 5-quart heavy pot over medium-low heat. When the pot is hot, add the remaining 2 tablespoons oil. When the oil is hot, add the ground mole sauce, the chocolate, and 1 cup of the reserved broth. Cook, stirring constantly, until the chocolate has melted and become fully integrated. The sauce should be the thickness of a thick milkshake; add more broth if needed.

8 Add the chicken to the sauce and cook, stirring often, until the chicken is heated through and becomes melded with the sauce, about 15 minutes. If the sauce has thickened too much, add a bit more broth. Allow the dish to rest for 15 minutes. Serve warm, not hot, with tortillas.

Carnitas Sandwiches with Árbol Chile Sauce

Tortas Ahogadas

Tortas, "sandwiches," are a Mexican street-food staple. This Guadalajara-style version (see photograph, page 121), the name of which literally translates to "drowned sandwiches," is the French dip's racy cousin, with Mexican-Style Pork Confit (page 193), also known as *carnitas*, rather than plain roast beef, a vivid tomato-based sauce instead of mild bouillon, and a garnish of pickled red onions. This recipe, based on one from La Chiva Come, a *fonda* in the Mixcoac neighborhood, is a welcome and substantial meal. You can substitute roast pork for the *carnitas*. Have the pork and pickled onions ready before you begin.

Makes 4 sandwiches

    2 tablespoons canola oil
    4 medium Roma tomatoes
    ½ medium white onion, quartered and
        separated into individual layers
    5 garlic cloves
    2 to 5 dried árbol chiles, stemmed
    5 whole allspice berries
    1 whole clove
    Pinch of ground cumin
    4 bay leaves
    1 teaspoon dried oregano
    ½ teaspoon dried thyme
    Freshly ground black pepper
    1 cup water
    2 tablespoons cider vinegar
    Salt
    1 stale baguette, quartered crosswise
        and each quarter split horizontally
    About 3½ cups Mexican-Style Pork Confit,
        shredded or cut into bite-size pieces
        (about 1¼ pounds; page 193)
    ½ cup Pickled Red Onions (page 199)

1 To make the sauce, heat a 12-inch skillet over medium heat. When the pan is hot, add 1 tablespoon of the oil. When the oil is hot, add the tomatoes and cook, turning often, until their skin blisters and cracks, about 7 minutes; if the oil splatters excessively, cover the skillet with a lid. Transfer the tomatoes to a plate. Add the white onion and garlic to the oil remaining in the pan and cook over medium heat, stirring constantly, until they just begin to pick up golden spots, about 4 minutes. Add the chiles, allspice, clove, cumin, bay leaves, oregano, thyme, and ¼ teaspoon pepper and cook, stirring constantly, until very fragrant, about 3 minutes.

2 Transfer the contents of the skillet to a blender, add the tomatoes, water, vinegar, and ½ teaspoon salt, and blend until smooth. Taste for salt and add more if needed. Strain the sauce through a fine-mesh sieve back into the skillet; discard the solids. Return the pan to medium-low heat, bring the sauce to a simmer, and simmer until reduced by about half, about 10 minutes. Keep the sauce hot while you assemble the sandwiches.

3 Warm the pork. To assemble the sandwiches, drench the interior side of each piece of bread directly into hot sauce, and place them cut-side up in individual soup bowls. Place a portion of the pork, then a portion of the pickled onions, onto each bottom piece of bread. Drench the top half of each bread quarter with more sauce. Close the sandwiches and pour extra sauce on top—you want them to be quite soupy. Serve at once with knives and forks.

Casa Virginia's Roasted Lamb with Pasilla Chiles
Pierna de Cordero con Pasilla

This recipe for fall-apart-tender roast lamb with a charred pasilla chile crust resembles a dish from the excellent Casa Virginia restaurant. It comes from executive chef Corentin Bertrand, and chef-owner Mónica Patiño. It is served accompanied by scalloped potatoes and garnished with nasturtium flowers and sea salt. This recipe calls for leg of lamb, but shoulder (see photograph, page 126) works well too; either way, give it at least 3 hours to marinate.

Serves 4

1 teaspoon ground ginger
1 teaspoon ground coriander
1 teaspoon plus pinch of ground cumin
1 teaspoon ground cinnamon
½ cup honey
1 tablespoon extra-virgin olive oil
Salt and freshly ground black pepper
One 8-pound bone-in leg of lamb or one 6-pound
    boneless leg of lamb, trimmed of excess fat
1 medium white onion, thickly sliced
1 cup Mexican Chicken Broth (page 194),
    plus more if needed
2 garlic cloves
7 pasilla chiles, 3 stemmed and seeded,
    4 left whole

1 To marinate the lamb, in a bowl, whisk together the ginger, coriander, 1 teaspoon of the cumin, the cinnamon, honey, oil, 1 teaspoon salt, and a few grinds of pepper. Using a knife or a skewer, poke about thirty holes into the meat, spacing them evenly over the entire surface. Coat the meat completely with the marinade, massage it into the holes, then place it in a large covered bowl and refrigerate for at least 3 hours or preferably overnight.

2 Preheat the oven to 350°F. Remove the lamb from the refrigerator. Using a roasting pan with a lid large enough to accommodate it, put the lamb into the pan, scatter the onion and garlic around it, then pour the broth over it. Cover and cook for 1½ hours; if you don't have a roasting pan with a lid, improvise and cover the pan tightly with aluminum foil. After 1½ hours, remove the lid and continue to cook, turning the meat every 30 minutes, for 1 hour and 40 minutes longer.

3 During the last 30 minutes or so of cooking, fill a medium bowl with hot water. Heat a 12-inch skillet over medium heat. When the pan is hot, add the stemmed and seeded chiles and cook, turning them frequently, until the surface softens slightly and they become fragrant, about 2 minutes. Transfer the chiles to the hot water and soak until they soften, about 10 minutes. Transfer the softened chiles to a blender along with ½ cup of their soaking water, add the remaining pinch of cumin and ½ teaspoon salt, and blend until smooth. Place the sauce into a bowl, then taste for salt, adding more if needed.

4 When the liquid in the roasting pan has evaporated, using a spoon, smear the sauce evenly over the lamb, including the underside. Raise the oven temperature to 500°F and cook uncovered until the sauce has created a thin crust on the surface of the meat, about 10 minutes. Meanwhile, place the whole chiles directly on the oven rack and roast them until they puff up, about 2 minutes.

5 Remove the lamb and chiles from the oven. Cover the lamb and let rest for 15 minutes. Carve the lamb and transfer the slices to a serving platter, garnished with the roasted chiles. Invite diners to break up the chiles and eat the flesh and seeds along with their lamb.

Pork Loin with Guajillo Chile Sauce
Lomo Adobado

Roasts made in chile-based sauces are frequently featured as the centerpiece of a Mexico City lunch (see photograph, page 135). The sauce here, made with three different varieties of dried chiles along with beer and spices, starts out liquidy but condenses as it cooks, until it is so thick it can be spread with a knife (and so delicious it's tempting to slather it directly onto a hot corn tortilla—so serve this dish with a stack of them, preferably homemade, page 196).

Serves 6

  5 bay leaves
  6 thyme sprigs, or ½ teaspoon dried thyme
  3 tablespoons extra-virgin olive oil
  5 garlic cloves, 1 clove coarsely chopped, 4 cloves whole and unpeeled
  2 teaspoons red or white wine vinegar
  Salt and freshly ground black pepper
  One 2½-pound boneless pork loin
  4 guajillo chiles, stemmed and seeded
  3 ancho chiles, stemmed and seeded
  3 pasilla chiles, stemmed and seeded
  ½ medium white onion, quartered and separated into individual layers
  ½ medium Roma tomato
  Generous pinch of ground cumin
  Generous pinch of aniseeds (optional)
  5 whole allspice berries
  2 whole cloves
  1 teaspoon dried oregano
  ¼ teaspoon ground cinnamon
  2 cups light or dark beer

1 At least 2 hours before you are ready to cook the pork or up to overnight, in a large nonreactive bowl, stir together the bay leaves, thyme, oil, the chopped garlic, 1 teaspoon of the vinegar, and ½ teaspoon each of salt and pepper. Add the pork, coat it evenly, cover and refrigerate.

2 When you're ready to cook the meat, prepare the sauce. Fill a bowl with hot water. Heat a 12-inch skillet over medium heat. When the pan is hot, add all of the chiles and cook until their surface softens slightly and they become fragrant, about 2 minutes. Transfer the chiles to the hot water and soak until they soften, about 10 minutes. Drain and set the chiles aside.

3 Meanwhile, while the pan is still hot (but without oil), add the onion and whole garlic cloves and toast, turning them as needed, until they begin to pick up dark spots on all sides, about 3 minutes. Set aside; peel the garlic once it is cool enough to handle. Add the tomato half, skin side down, to the hot skillet and cook on the skin side only, moving it occasionally to prevent burning, until the skin begins to blister and pick up dark spots, about 3 minutes. Remove from the heat.

4 In a blender, combine the softened chiles, onion, and garlic, the remaining 1 teaspoon vinegar, the cumin, aniseeds (if using), allspice, cloves, oregano, cinnamon, 1 teaspoon salt, and ½ cup of the beer. Blend until smooth, adding the remaining 1½ cups beer in increments to keep the ingredients moving in the blender. Taste for salt, adding more if needed.

5 Preheat the oven to 300°F. At least half an hour before cooking the pork, remove it from the refrigerator. Put the pork and its marinade in a roasting pan with a lid large enough to accommodate the pork loin and pour the sauce evenly all over it. Cover and cook for 1 hour, checking occasionally to make sure neither the sauce nor the meat is scorching (if it is, mix a tablespoon or two of water into the sauce to thin it a bit). After 1 hour, turn the meat over, re-cover, and continue cooking for 1 hour longer. Uncover, turn the pork over one more time, and cook until the sauce is a bit thicker than applesauce, about 15 minutes longer.

6 Remove the pork from the oven and let it rest covered for 15 minutes before serving.

Stuffed Roasted Poblano Chiles with Walnut Sauce
Chiles en Nogada

This elaborate preparation of poblano chiles (see photograph, page 137), stuffed with nearly twenty ingredients and blanketed with a smooth sauce made of goat cheese and ground walnuts, comes from Puebla, a neighboring city celebrated for its baroque European-influenced cooking style. Serving the dish at room temperature is essential to fully experience the flavor balance.

Serves 10

3 cups walnut halves

1½ cups blanched whole almonds, plus 2 cups minced

About 3 cups whole milk

10 medium poblano chiles, 4 to 5 inches long, with stems intact

¼ cup canola oil

1 medium white onion, minced

6 large garlic cloves, minced

8 medium Roma tomatoes, minced

1¼ cups loosely packed fresh flat-leaf parsley leaves, minced

8 ounces ground beef

8 ounces ground pork

Salt and freshly ground black pepper

1½ teaspoons ground cinnamon

½ teaspoon ground cloves

5 whole allspice berries, finely ground

½ cup minced black or golden raisins

½ cup minced candied fruit (such as citron or pineapple; see page 158)

⅓ cup pine nuts, finely chopped

1 large sweet apple (such as Golden Delicious or Gala), peeled, cored, and minced

1 medium pear (such as Bosc or Bartlett), cored and minced

2 firm small peaches, pitted and minced

1 very ripe small plantain (about 8 inches), peeled and minced

¾ cup fresh goat cheese

¾ cup dry sherry

2½ cups water

5 teaspoons sugar

1 medium pomegranate, seeded

1 In a bowl, combine the walnuts, the 1½ cups whole almonds, and enough milk to cover the nuts. Cover and refrigerate until you are ready to make the sauce.

2 Roast the poblanos as directed on page 196. Then, using kitchen shears, cut a lengthwise slit in each chile, leaving about ½ inch uncut at the stem end and at the bottom. Remove the seeds and membranes and discard; work carefully, as it is important the chiles remain whole. Wipe the chiles well with paper towels. Sprinkle a pinch of salt inside each chile, then set them aside at room temperature.

3 To make the stuffing, heat a 12-inch (preferably larger, if you have one) skillet over medium-low heat. When the pan is hot, add the oil. When the oil is hot, add the ingredients as instructed, stirring often throughout the following process: Add the onion and cook until translucent, about 5 minutes. Add the garlic and cook until softened, about 3 minutes. Add the tomatoes and 1 cup of the parsley and cook until the tomatoes have broken down and their liquid has mostly evaporated, about 15 minutes. Raise the heat to medium, add the beef, pork, 1½ teaspoons salt, and ½ teaspoon pepper and cook, breaking up any large clumps of meat with a wooden spoon, until the meat is cooked through and nearly all of the liquid in the pan has evaporated, 10 to 15 minutes. Add the 2 cups minced almonds, the cinnamon, ¼ teaspoon of the cloves, the allspice, raisins, candied fruit, and pine nuts and cook for 5 minutes. Add the apple and cook for 4 minutes. Add the pear and cook for 3 minutes. Add the peach and cook for 3 minutes. Finally, add the plantain and cook for 3 minutes. Turn down the heat to low and cook until all of the ingredients are well combined and the mixture is dry, 1 to 2 minutes longer. Taste for salt and add more if needed. Transfer the stuffing to a large bowl and set aside.

4 To make the sauce, drain the walnuts and whole almonds, discarding the milk, and add them to a blender along with the goat cheese, sherry, water, the remaining ¼ teaspoon cloves, the sugar, and 2 teaspoons salt. Blend until smooth and the consistency of a milkshake; you may need to do this in two batches. Taste for salt, adding more if needed. Set aside.

5 Stuff a chile well with the fruit-meat mixture, being sure to stuff every part of the chile, until the chile is quite full. Set the stuffed chile aside. Repeat with the remaining chiles. If any filling is left over, save it for eating as a side dish.

6 Place a stuffed chile, seam side down, in the center of each individual plate. Ladle about ¾ cup of the sauce over the chile—you want the sauce to fully cover the chile without drowning it. Sprinkle about 1 tablespoon of the pomegranate seeds and about 1 teaspoon of the remaining parsley over each sauced chile. Repeat with the remaining chiles. Serve at room temperature.

Milanesa-Style Beef Burgers
Milanesas de Carne Molida

A *comida* (lunchtime) favorite, this is a very thin beef patty (see photograph, page 145, top left) that has been breaded and panfried until golden and a little crisp. It's a secret weapon of busy cooks who want to provide something quick and substantial. Serve with warm tortillas and your favorite salsa.

Makes 8 patties

1 pound ground beef
1 egg, lightly beaten
2 tablespoons coarsely chopped fresh flat-leaf parsley leaves
¾ cup fine dried bread crumbs
Salt and freshly ground black pepper
Canola oil, for frying

1 In a medium bowl, combine the beef, egg, parsley, ¼ cup of the bread crumbs, ¼ teaspoon salt, and a few grinds of pepper and mix until all the ingredients are evenly distributed. Spread the remaining ½ cup bread crumbs on a plate, sprinkle with ¼ teaspoon salt and a couple of grinds of pepper, and mix together.

2 Scoop up 3 tablespoons at a time of the meat mixture and form into very thin, round patties about 3 inches in diameter and ¼ inch thick. Press each side of the patties into the seasoned bread crumbs, creating a crust on both sides. Set the patties aside. You should have 8 patties total.

3 Line a platter with paper towels. Heat a 12-inch skillet over medium heat. When the pan is hot, add about 1½ tablespoons of the oil. When the oil is hot, working in batches and adding more oil to the pan as needed, add as many patties as will comfortably fit in the pan and fry, turning once, until a delicate golden brown on both sides, about 2 minutes on each side. As they are ready, transfer them to the platter. Serve at once.

Meatballs in Chipotle-Mint Broth
Albóndigas

These springy-textured meatballs (see photograph, page 145, top right) are cooked with vegetables in a broth seasoned with thyme, chipotle, and mint. The recipe is inspired by one from the grandmother of Itzia Fernández, a documentary filmmaker native to Mexico City.

Serves 6

1 medium white onion

5 small carrots

3 small zucchini

8 ounces ground beef

8 ounces ground pork

3 tablespoons minced fresh flat-leaf parsley

1 egg, lightly beaten, plus 3 hard-cooked eggs, peeled and cut into sixths

¼ cup fine dried bread crumbs

Salt and freshly ground black pepper

2 medium Roma tomatoes

6 garlic cloves, unpeeled

1 tablespoon extra-virgin olive oil

9 cups Mexican Chicken Broth (page 194)

3 bay leaves

3 thyme sprigs, or ¼ teaspoon dried thyme

5 peppermint or spearmint sprigs

3 chipotle chiles, stems intact

Avocado slices, for serving

Corn tortillas, homemade (page 196) or store-bought, warmed, or hot cooked white rice, for serving

1 Halve the onion, then mince half; quarter the remaining half, and separate the quarters into individual layers. Peel the carrots, then, through the largest hole on a grater, grate three carrots (about 2 cups) and cut the remaining two carrots crosswise into ⅓-inch-thick slices (about 1 cup). Through the largest hole on a grater, grate one zucchini (about ¾ cup) and cut the remaining two zucchini into ⅓-inch-thick slices (about 1 cup).

2 To make the meatballs, in a large bowl, combine the beef, pork, parsley, beaten egg, bread crumbs, 2 teaspoons salt, ½ teaspoon pepper, the minced onion, grated carrot, and grated zucchini. Mix well. To shape each meatball, scoop up 3 tablespoons of the meat mixture and roll between your palms into a firm ball. With your index finger, make a well in the center of the ball. Place one piece of hard-cooked egg into the well and reshape the meat into a firm ball, enclosing the egg piece. Set aside. Repeat until

all of the meat mixture and hard-cooked egg pieces are used. You should have 18 meatballs.

3 Heat a large skillet over medium heat. When the pan is hot, place the tomatoes, garlic, and remaining half onion onto the pan and grill, turning them with tongs just once or twice on each side, until all of the ingredients have picked up some charred spots, 10 to 20 minutes. As the vegetables are ready, peel the garlic, and transfer the tomatoes, onion, and garlic to a blender. Grind the ingredients until the mixture is smooth.

4 Heat a large, heavy pot over medium heat. When the pot is hot, add the oil, then strain the tomato-onion-garlic mixture through a fine-mesh sieve directly into the pot; discard the solids. Simmer the sauce, stirring often, until it no longer tastes raw, about 5 minutes. Add the broth, bay leaves, thyme, mint, and chipotles, turn up the heat, and bring to a boil. Carefully add the meatballs, one at a time, to the broth. Allow the liquid to come to a boil again, then turn down the heat to medium-low. Cover and cook at a steady, gentle simmer until the meatballs are firm, about 30 minutes.

5 Add the carrot slices, re-cover, and cook until they are just fork-tender, about 15 minutes longer. Add the zucchini slices, re-cover, and cook until they are quite tender, about 20 minutes longer. Taste the broth, adding salt if needed. Test a meatball to see if it is cooked through.

6 Allow three meatballs for each diner, spooning them into shallow bowls and topping them with a couple of ladles of broth and vegetables. Serve hot, with avocado slices and warm tortillas on the side. Alternatively, spoon each serving of meatballs, broth, and vegetables over a big scoop of rice.

Clockwise from top left: Milanesa-Style Burgers (page 143); Meatballs in Chipotle-Mint Broth (page 143); Guadalajara-Style Beef and Bean Stew (page 147); Spice-Braised Beef Stew with Anchos and Guajillos (page 146).

Spice-Braised Beef Stew with Anchos and Guajillos

Adobo de la Abuela Fina

This stew (see photograph, page 145, bottom left), in which dried chiles and spices are ground to a paste and added to an already tender braise of beef, is a perfect dinner main course. The recipe is based on one by Alberto Estúa, who, with his husband, Jorge Fitz, runs the marvelous Mexico City cooking school Casa Jacaranda. To do the dish justice, use good-quality beef chuck—not precut "beef stew." Drunken Rice (page 37) makes just the right side dish.

Serves 4

  2 pounds boneless beef chuck or tenderloin, cut into 2-inch pieces
  1 white onion, quartered
  3 garlic cloves (1 unpeeled)
  3 bay leaves
  3 thyme sprigs (optional)
  Salt
  5 ancho chiles, stemmed and seeded
  3 guajillo chiles, stemmed and seeded
  3 Roma tomatoes
  3 whole cloves
  5 whole allspice berries
  ¼ teaspoon ground cinnamon
  Pinch of ground cumin
  Pinch of dried thyme
  1½ teaspoons sugar
  1 tablespoon canola oil

1 In a large pot, combine the beef, one-quarter of the onion, the two peeled garlic cloves, two of the bay leaves, the thyme sprigs (if using), 1 teaspoon salt, and cold water to cover by 2 inches, and stir to dissolve the salt. Bring to a boil over high heat, turn down the heat to medium, cover partially, and cook, stirring occasionally and skimming off any foam that forms, until the meat is extremely tender, about 2½ hours. If the level of the liquid falls below the meat, add hot water as needed to cover. Drain the contents of the pot through a fine-mesh sieve into a bowl.

Remove the meat; discard the remaining solids. Measure 1½ cups of the broth for the stew; reserve the remaining broth for another use or discard. Set the meat and broth aside.

2 While the meat cooks, make the adobo sauce. Have ready a medium bowl of hot water. Heat a 12-inch skillet or comal over medium heat. When the pan is hot, add all of the chiles and cook, turning them frequently, until they are lightly toasted on all sides and fragrant, about 2 minutes. Transfer the chiles to the hot water and soak until they have softened, about 10 minutes.

3 Return the skillet or comal to medium heat. When the pan is hot, place the tomatoes, the remaining three-quarters onion, and the unpeeled garlic onto the pan and grill, turning them with tongs just once or twice on each side, until all of the ingredients have picked up some charred spots, 10 to 20 minutes, depending on the vegetable. As the tomatoes and onion are ready, set aside on a plate; peel the garlic and place on the plate. Put the remaining bay leaf, the cloves, allspice, cinnamon, cumin, and dried thyme in the skillet and pan-roast, stirring, until fragrant, about 1 minute.

4 Drain the chiles, discarding the water. In a blender, combine the chiles; the charred onion, garlic, and tomatoes; the toasted herbs and spices; the sugar; ½ teaspoon salt; and the 1½ cups reserved broth and blend until smooth.

5 Heat a large, heavy pot over medium heat. When the pot is hot, add the oil. Pour in the chile mixture (watch out, as it will splatter), add the beef, and bring to a simmer. Cook at a steady simmer, stirring often, until the beef has melded with the sauce, about 20 minutes.

6 Taste for salt, adding more if needed. Serve hot.

Guadalajara-Style Beef and Bean Stew

Carne en su Jugo

This hearty and comforting stew of beef and white beans (see photograph, page 145, bottom right) gets its soul from a tomatillo-and-serrano seasoning base and the smoky appeal of bacon. It's generally eaten with hot tortillas, but a baguette works just as well for soaking up the delicious sauce.

Serves 4

   4 slices bacon (about 4 ounces),
      cut into ½-inch pieces
   2 tablespoons canola oil, if needed
   2½ medium white onions, 1 onion finely
      chopped, 1 onion coarsely chopped,
      and ½ onion minced, for garnish
   6 garlic cloves, 3 cloves finely chopped,
      3 cloves coarsely chopped
   1 pound flank steak, very thinly sliced against
      the grain, then cut into 1-inch pieces
   Salt
   3 thyme sprigs, or ¼ teaspoon dried thyme
   4 medium tomatillos, husks removed, rinsed,
      and quartered
   1 to 3 serrano chiles, stemmed and
      coarsely chopped
   1 cup loosely packed cilantro sprigs with
      2-inch stems, coarsely chopped
   2 cups peruano or Great Northern beans,
      home cooked (see page 192) or canned,
      drained and rinsed
   3 limes, quartered, for serving

1 Heat a large, heavy pot over medium-low heat. When the pot is hot, add the bacon and cook, stirring, until most of its fat has rendered, about 5 minutes. If the bacon is very lean, add up to 2 tablespoons oil to keep it from scorching. Add the finely chopped onion and cook until translucent, stirring often, for 4 minutes. Add the finely chopped garlic and cook, stirring often, until it is soft, about 3 minutes. Turn up the heat to medium, add the beef and ½ teaspoon salt,

and cook, stirring often, until the beef begins to brown, about 3 minutes; raise the heat slightly if the meat is not browning. Add the thyme, stir well, and turn down the heat to its lowest possible level. Cover and cook, stirring occasionally, for 1 to 1½ hours. If the liquid evaporates, add hot water, ½ cup at a time, until the water is about ¼ inch deep in the bottom of the pot.

2 Meanwhile, make the seasoning. In a blender, combine the tomatillos, serrano (adjusting the amount to your taste), ½ cup of the cilantro, the coarsely chopped onion, the coarsely chopped garlic, and ½ teaspoon salt. Blend until smooth.

3 Add the tomatillo mixture to the pot, mix well, then cover and cook, stirring occasionally, for 1 hour or until the meat is very tender when tested. Add the beans (and any liquid if home cooked), mix well, and heat through, about 10 minutes. Taste for salt, and add more if needed. Remove from the heat, cover, and let rest for 10 minutes before serving.

4 Ladle the stew onto individual bowls. Top each serving with the minced onion and the remaining cilantro. Pass the lime quarters at the table for squeezing into the stew just before eating.

Green Mole with Chicken

Mole Verde Con Pollo

Mole verde (page 133) is a form of mole that uses a variety of vegetables instead of the dried chiles, fruits, and seeds of Milpa Alta Chicken Mole (page 138). This version was inspired by Beatriz de la Rosa, a home cook originally from the state of Guanajuato.

Serves 6 to 8

   3 bone-in, skin-on chicken thighs
   3 bone-in, skin-on chicken drumsticks
   4 whole allspice berries
   3 bay leaves
   4 cilantro sprigs
   1 medium white onion, quartered

6 garlic cloves

Salt

6 medium tomatillos, husks removed, rinsed,
and quartered

1½ cups raw shelled pepitas (see page 199)

5 green onions, top 1 inch of green tops
discarded, then coarsely chopped

1 poblano chile, stemmed, seeded, and cut
into coarse chunks

1 to 3 jalapeño chiles, stemmed, seeded,
and cut into coarse chunks

8 medium Swiss chard leaves, bottom 1 inch
of stems discarded, then coarsely chopped

1 cup loosely packed cilantro leaves and stems,
coarsely chopped

¾ cup loosely packed fresh flat-leaf parsley
leaves, coarsely chopped

½ cup loosely packed fresh epazote leaves
(see page 198), coarsely chopped (optional)

¼ cup canola oil

Corn tortillas, homemade (page 196) or
store-bought, warmed, for serving

1 In a large pot, combine the chicken, allspice, bay leaves, cilantro, onion, two of the garlic cloves, and 2 teaspoons salt. Add water to cover by 1 to 2 inches and stir to dissolve the salt. Bring to a boil over high heat, turn down the heat to medium, and cook, maintaining a steady simmer, stirring occasionally, and skimming off any foam that forms on the surface, until the chicken is cooked through, 30 to 35 minutes. Using tongs or a wire skimmer, transfer the chicken to a large plate. Strain the broth through a fine-mesh sieve into a bowl and discard the solids; reserve the strained broth.

2 In a medium saucepan, cover the tomatillos with water to cover by 1 inch and bring to a boil. Turn down the heat to medium-low and simmer until the tomatillos have turned from bright green to drab olive and can be easily punctured with a fork, about 7 minutes. Drain and set aside.

3 Heat a 12-inch skillet over medium heat. Add the pepitas and the remaining four garlic cloves and cook, stirring constantly, until the pepitas begin to toast and become fragrant and the garlic begins to pick up golden spots, about 6 minutes. Set them aside to cool slightly, then add them to a food processor and pulse until ground to a powdery consistency, as fine as possible. Transfer the mixture to a small bowl and set aside.

4 Add to the food processor the tomatillos, green onions, poblano, jalapeño (adjusting the amount to your taste), Swiss chard, cilantro, parsley, and epazote (if using) and process until the consistency of a thick milkshake; you may need to do this in two batches. If the mixture is too thick, gradually add up to 1 cup of the reserved broth to thin it. Set this mixture aside.

5 In a 5-quart heavy pot, heat the oil over medium heat. Add the ground pepita-garlic mixture and cook, stirring constantly, until it begins to darken and become fragrant, about 3 minutes. Stir in the tomatillo mixture, mixing well. Taste for salt, adding more if needed. Bring to a lazy boil, then turn down the heat to low and simmer just until you notice signs of thickening, about 5 minutes. Add 1 cup of the reserved broth, mix well, and simmer until the sauce darkens slightly and tastes deep and vegetal rather than raw, about 15 minutes. The sauce will continue to thicken, but if it gets thicker than a thick milkshake, stir in more broth, ½ cup at a time. Add the cooked chicken and heat through, 5 to 10 minutes longer.

6 Allow the dish to rest for 15 minutes. Serve warm, not hot, with the tortillas.

Calle Regina in Centro Histórico.

7

Los Dulceros

Desserts and Sweets

Lulú de la Cruz, a genteel and gracious yoga instructor, is an accomplished home cook in general, but she particularly excels at sweets. Her daughter, journalist Margot Castañeda, is coming over for dinner tonight, and de la Cruz is mostly ready; all that's left is to decide what to make for dessert.

"I'm looking forward to seeing you," she tells her daughter on the phone. "I have sweet potatoes; I was thinking I'd make camotes en piloncillo, and we could have it with vanilla ice cream. What do you say?"

"That sounds nice. But would you consider making—"

"Let me guess. Capirotada?"

"Yes, please!" Castañeda exclaims.

De la Cruz smiles. Castañeda is in her early thirties and is a magazine editor with a fully adult and independent life, yet her mother's cooking can still induce guileless excitement. De la Cruz is originally from that grand colonial bastion of art and culture, Morelia, the capital of Michoacán, and her recipe for *capirotada*, a savory-sweet bread dessert that combines European and Mexican flavors, is typically Morelian. Moreover, her mother and her mother's grandmother used to make it. Being a person who appreciates upholding tradition, she loves that it has been her daughter's favorite thing to eat since she was old enough to hold a fork.

Her daughter is certainly not alone in her zeal for dessert. As evidenced by the roving candy stores that roll down the sidewalks, a lust for sugar is a major component of everyday life in Mexico City.

Collective sweet tooth aside, that passion for sugar is intrinsic to the city's religious traditions, too. People the world over are familiar with the sight of the glittering sugar skulls made during the Day of the Dead to honor one's ancestors, and that is but one of the goodies prepared on that holiday. The occasion also brings forth *pan de muerto*, a brioche-like bun flavored with anise and orange flower water, often decorated with bone- and teardrop-shaped dough. A different sweet bread is made for Epiphany: *rosca de reyes* (king's cake), decorated with crystallized fruit and bearing a baked-in figurine of the infant Jesus.

The ancient Mexican sweeteners were honey and agave syrup, the latter made from the nectar of the maguey (the plant that yields mezcal) and available in differing grades, from a mildly sweet colorless liquid to a rich brown caramel-flavored syrup. With the Spanish Conquest came sugarcane, adapted into *piloncillo* cones, compressed raw sugar with a golden-brown color and a molasses-like flavor. From it we get such traditional foods as *camotes en piloncillo*, sweet potatoes simmered until tender with orange peel and cinnamon—the dessert de la Cruz was originally considering.

In the areas around street-food stalls, which don't typically serve dessert, strolling merchants tote wicker baskets full of traditional candies sold for a few pesos apiece. Other candies nestled within include chewy squares of grated coconut and *jamoncillo*, a toothache-sweet fudge made by boiling down sweet spiced milk. Tamarind is stewed into a sour paste, then doused in chile powder, and peanuts are made into halvah-like candies called *mazapanes* (fun tip: these can be blended with whole milk or ice cream to make an addictive peanut-flavored milkshake). Tucked next to the mazapanes might be *alegrías*, bars of amaranth and sunflower seeds bound together with sticky piloncillo syrup. The name *alegría* says it all: "happiness."

Of the Mexico City shops that sell traditional Mexican confections, the queen of them all is Dulcería de Celaya in Centro, which carries all the old-time candies and then some. Its high ceilings and tiled floors speak of civility and manners, and to enter its cool hush—and be lured by its glass cases displaying sweet treasures from all over the country, from caramels to candied guavas from Puebla—is an experience that no visitor should miss. Additionally, every neighborhood has its *panaderías*, or baked-goods take-out shops, selling bread and pastries to be eaten first thing in the morning with coffee or hot chocolate, or late in the evening for a sweet supper (or straight from the bag on the way home).

Page 150: Spiced Sweet Potatoes with Mexican Brown Sugar (page 172).

A fruit vendor at Mercado
Portales. Pages 154 to 155:
fruit cups, which are sold as
a snack throughout the city.

The antidote to all of this temptation? Mexico City's other form of sweet consumption: fresh fruit. Although the city's own altitudinous climate is relatively cool, tropical environs are found just a couple of hundred miles away (to comprehend this extremity, imagine if New York City and Honolulu were a couple of hundred miles apart). For this reason, the city's fruit reigns supreme. Strawberries, the subtle-tasting tuna fruit of the nopal cactus, papayas with bright orange flesh from the state of Colima—whatever you fancy can be cut for you by a fruit vendor. Most fruits are served plain, though you might like a peeled slice of mango or watermelon sprinkled with ground chile and salt.

Preserving Summer's Sweetness

Candying fresh fruit is an important culinary tradition in Mexico. Candied fruit is eaten as as a treat on its own, used in certain savory recipes such as Stuffed Roasted Poblano Chiles with Walnut Sauce (page 142) to add crunch and color, and baked into the breads eaten on King's Day and the Day of the Dead holidays. To make it, fruit is cooked, whole or cut, in a sugar syrup until the cooking process has extracted much of the water from the fruit and generously coated its exterior, leaving it soft and glittering with crystallization. All manner of fruit is treated in this way, from pumpkin and fig and quince, to pear on the stem, to cactus fruit and papaya, to every possible variety of citrus, some plain and some deliciously inventive, like limes stuffed with grated sweetened coconut. Street vendors and markets arrange tempting technicolor spreads of these *frutas cristalizadas*, offering both a feast for the eyes and a preview of the luscious flavors.

Back in de la Cruz's kitchen, she fries baguette slices until they're crisp and then makes a fragrant syrup of melted *piloncillo* cones, star anise, cloves, allspice, and, curiously, bay leaves and tomato, which lend surprising intrigue. After buttering the heavy white casserole dish her daughter knows so well, she layers the fried bread, syrup, raisins, and, lastly, a handful of crumbled Cotija, a semisoft, salty cheese named for a Michoacán town.

Later that evening, as she watches her daughter enjoying the dish, de la Cruz says, "Margot, my love, some traditions are too delicious to resist."

"For many from Michoacán, the state where I was born, capirotada is a dessert, breakfast, snack, even a complete meal—a cozy, inexpensive dish that fills our bellies and brings the family together. In my childhood home, we'd share it from the same container, without plates, and for me it is still a joyous food."

—LULÚ DE LA CRUZ, YOGA INSTRUCTOR; RECIPE ON PAGE 172

Sweet Heaven

Founded in 1927, Pastelería Ideal went from being a modest baked-goods shop to being a Mexico City icon. For the residents here, the bakery's staggeringly diverse sweet breads—most designed to be dipped into a mug of morning or evening coffee or hot chocolate—have become part and parcel of daily city life. It doesn't matter whether one lives far from one of their two (always jam-packed) Centro Histórico locations; sweets from the bakery reach every corner of the city via a fleet of traveling vendors who, hauling baskets and boxes on their bicycles, transport La Ideal's pastry to groggy commuters hungry for a little something before they face the day's work. But as with many things in life, the bakery's treats are not something to be sampled only once. The best way to conclude the day is to look for one of those bike-riding vendors on the way home—recognizable by their cargo of La Ideal's signature string-wrapped boxes—and savor another piece of sugary paradise. —*Pablo Orube*

Delivery people transport pastries from Pastelería Ideal to locations across the city by bike.

An employee on break at Pastelería Ideal. Having served Mexico City for nearly a hundred years, the bakery has become intrinsic to city life.

Treasured wild honey in Milpa Alta. Opposite: Flan (page 174), bathed in caramelized sugar.

①

②

③

④

⑤

⑥

Something to Sweeten Your Day

Street vendors sell treats like these out of baskets like the one shown, offering an array of *dulces de coco*, milk fudge, crystallized fruits, chocolates, and more. A simple and positively addictive mixture of finely ground peanuts and confectioners' sugar, **mazapanes** ① (a play on the word *marzipan*) are crumbly, nutty pastilles sold in abundance, particularly the de la Rosa brand. Rainbow-hued **obleas** ② are made of the same superfine flour as communion wafers, but there the resemblance ends. They are stuffed with a layer of *cajeta*, a goat-milk caramel, and crowned with *pepitas* (pumpkin seeds). For those seeking the flavors of tamarindo con chile in its packaged form, **Pulparindo** ③ is the best-selling brand. **Alegrías de amaranto** ④ are made of puffy, crispy amaranth seeds bound together with piloncillo syrup; they are often bolstered with peanuts or sunflower seeds. A combination of tart, hot, and sweet flavors is a signature of Mexico City sweets, and **tamarindo con chile** ⑤, tamarind and sugar paste dredged in piquant chile and salt, has it in spades. Moist and very sweet, candied cactus fruit, or **ate de tuna** ⑥, is just one of the countless ways the native nopal cactus has earned its place as an edible national treasure. Coconut and sugar combine to make bars of chewy-sweet **dulces de coco** ⑦. Flavored with cinnamon, vanilla, and almond, tablets of **Mexican chocolate** ⑧ are not only dissolved in hot water or milk for a wonderful hot beverage but are also a terrific eating chocolate. Rich milk fudge flavored with pine nut essence is sold in candy bar form, as in the popular **Jessy brand** ⑨.

⑦

⑧

Dulces - Jessy -

INGREDIENTES:
LECHE DE VACA
AZUCAR
FRUTA DE PIÑON
ESENCIA DE PIÑON
COLOR ARTIFICIAL
SORBATO DE POTASIO
COMO CONSERVADOR

ELABORADO EN:
CHIGNAHUAPAN, PUE.
BLVD. GUSTAVO DÍAZ O. S/N
TEL. (01 797) 97 1 06 00
R.F.C. HELD9412294N4

⑨

Spiced Sweet Potatoes with Mexican Brown Sugar

Camotes en Piloncillo

In this dish (see photograph, page 150), sweet potato slices are poached in a syrup of Mexican brown sugar, a match made in heaven. Eat it as is or with vanilla ice cream.

Serves 4

   Two 8-ounce piloncillo cones (see page 200)
   1 orange peel strip, 3 inches long by ½ inch wide
   1 star anise pod
   2 whole cloves
   3 whole allspice berries
   1 cinnamon stick, about 2 inches long, broken into small shards
   1½ cups water
   1 pound sweet potatoes, unpeeled, sliced crosswise ⅓ inch thick

1 In a large saucepan, combine the piloncillo, orange peel, star anise, cloves, allspice, cinnamon, and water and bring to a boil over high heat, stirring occasionally. Turn down the heat to medium-low, cover, and cook, stirring and poking the sugar with a spoon to help it dissolve occasionally, until the sugar has finally melted and the liquid is slightly syrupy, about 30 minutes.

2 Add the sweet potato slices, re-cover, and cook, turning the slices occasionally, until fork-tender, about 30 minutes. Remove from the heat and let cool for 10 minutes before serving.

Festive Bread Pudding with Mexican Brown Sugar

Capirotada

Traditionally eaten during Lent, this mélange of mostly sweet ingredients with just a hint of salty cheese is scrumptious: fried bread studded with raisins and drenched in an aromatic syrup. The recipe is inspired by one from Lulú de la Cruz.

Serves 6

   Two 8-ounce piloncillo cones (see page 200)
   1 star anise pod
   2 whole cloves
   3 whole allspice berries
   3 bay leaves
   1 Roma tomato, quartered
   1 cup water
   About 1½ cups canola oil
   55 to 60 slightly stale baguette slices, each ¼ inch thick (about 1⅓ average-sized baguettes)
   ¾ cup black or golden raisins
   1 cup finely crumbled Cojita (see page 193) or other aged dry Mexican cheese

1 In a large saucepan, combine the piloncillo, star anise, cloves, allspice, bay leaves, tomato, and water and bring to a boil over high heat. Turn down the heat to medium-low and cook, uncovered, poking at the sugar with a spoon to help it break up, until the sugar has fully dissolved, about 30 minutes. Continue cooking, stirring often, until the liquid is syrupy—the consistency should be a little thinner than honey—about 15 minutes more. Remove from the heat and discard all the solid ingredients with a spoon; set syrup aside.

2 Line a large plate with paper towels. In a 12-inch skillet, heat ¾ cup of the oil over medium heat. When the oil is hot (to test it, drop in a small scrap of bread; if bubbles form around it instantly, the oil is ready), add as many baguette slices as will fit comfortably in a single layer and fry, turning once, until golden and crunchy, about 1 minute on each side. Set aside on the plate. Repeat with the remaining baguette slices, adding more oil as needed to keep the same level and adjusting the heat as necessary.

3 Butter an 11 by 8-inch baking dish (about 2-quart capacity) or serving platter with at least 2-inch sides, and arrange a layer of fried bread on the bottom. Drizzle about ½ cup of the syrup over the bread, then scatter a small

Opposite: Spiced Poached Strawberries (page 174). Pages 170 to 171: candy for sale.

handful each of the raisins and the cheese over the top, dispersing them evenly. Repeat the layers evenly—bread, syrup, raisins, cheese—until all of the ingredients are used up. Pour any remaining syrup over the top. Rest it for at least 15 minutes or up to an hour before serving.

Flan

A silky custard redolent with vanilla and cinnamon and topped with burnt-sugar syrup, flan (see photograph, page 166) is a luxurious treat that is simple to make. This Mexicanized cream cheese version of the classic Spanish dessert calls for a *flanera* (see page 197), a dedicated pan with a clamp-on lid, but you can improvise one by using a cake pan sealed tightly with aluminum foil.

Serves 6

½ cup sugar

One 12-ounce can evaporated milk

One 12-ounce can condensed milk

One 8-ounce package cream cheese,
    at room temperature

5 eggs, lightly beaten

1½ teaspoons pure vanilla extract

½ teaspoon ground cinnamon

1 In a flanera, heat the sugar over low heat, stirring constantly, just until it turns a deep golden brown and liquefies, about 7 minutes (it will foam at first). Immediately transfer the flanera to a level work surface and let stand undisturbed until a firm caramel shell forms on the sugar's surface, about 10 minutes.

2 In a blender, combine both milks, the cream cheese, eggs, vanilla, and cinnamon and blend until smooth. Set aside. Pour water to a depth of about ¾ inch into a wide pot or large skillet (the water level must be no deeper than half the height of the flanera) and bring it to a boil.

3 Pour the milk mixture into the caramel-lined flanera. Clamp on the cover. Gently place the flanera in the pot and cover the pot. Turn down the heat to low and cook until a toothpick

inserted into the center comes out clean, about 1 hour and 20 minutes. Periodically lift the lid of the pot to check on the water, and add hot water as needed to maintain the original level.

4 Uncover the pot, remove the flanera from the hot water, and let cool for 20 minutes, then refrigerate for 2 hours. Remove the cover, invert a round serving platter over the mold, and, holding the mold and platter together, swiftly flip them. Lift off the mold (you may need to shake the mold gently first). Cut into wedges and serve.

Spiced Poached Strawberries

Fresas en Jarabe Especiado

Strawberries star in this syrupy spice-and-wine-poached dish (see photograph, page 173). Eat it as is, serve it atop vanilla ice cream, or spoon it alongside Flan (see left).

Serves 4

2 tablespoons unsalted butter

5 tablespoons sugar

3 whole cloves

1-inch piece cinnamon stick

½ cup white wine or light red wine,
    such as Riesling or Pinot Noir

1½ pounds large fresh strawberries, hulled
    and halved lengthwise (about 5 cups)

¼ cup dry sherry

¼ cup tequila or Cointreau

1 Heat a 12-inch skillet over medium heat. When the pan is hot, add the butter and melt it, stirring constantly. Stir in the sugar, combine well, then stir in the cloves, cinnamon, and wine and cook at a lively simmer, stirring constantly, until the sugar is completely dissolved. Allow the liquid to cook until it is reduced by roughly half, about 5 minutes. Add the strawberries, sherry, and tequila and cook, turning them once, until they are just fork-tender, about 10 minutes. Serve at once.

The chapel of the Catedral Metropolitana, the city's most iconic place of worship.

8

A Thirst
for Life

Beverages

The scene at Las Duelistas,
where pulque, *a traditional
beverage made of the fermented
sap of the agave plant, is the
drink of choice. Page 176: a
tequila shot, served with lime.*

G uitars in hand, a mariachi band is entering Cantina la Reforma. The musicians are resplendent in their traditional Jalisco-style regalia of snug-fitting, extravagantly embroidered black suits and matching sombreros. Waiter Miguel Ángel Sánchez gives them a playful bow as they file in. Sánchez, in his own uniform of crisp shirt and apron, is a longtime employee at the cantina, which was originally on Mexico City's Paseo de la Reforma, in Centro Histórico. The place has relocated since then, but it stayed nearby, and it still has a wholesome feel to it, with its bright lighting and walls bedecked with murals depicting scenes of bullfighting and cathedrals, above which a television is showing a fútbol match. Hoarsely, the announcer cries, "GOOOOOOL!"

Sánchez glances at a young couple's table and heads for the kitchen. The couple hasn't finished their round of tequila, but they do need another botana. *Botanas* are house-made snacks served free with the price of drinks— a time-honored way to keep customers in one place. The last one Sánchez brought out for them, sliced cucumbers dusted with chile powder, they devoured immediately.

At the table where two generations are celebrating a girl's sixth birthday, the kids are horsing around, pausing to gulp their *aguas frescas*. These lucent, rainbow-hued beverages are an omnipresent refreshment in Mexico City. Served from glass jars or pitchers to showcase their color, they are made of water infused with fruit or vegetable juices; don't confuse them with juice, though. Agua frescas are a distinctly Mexican construct meant to add savor to a meal, not just quench thirst. The flavors—from tangy lime to nourishing cucumber and cooling mint—echo nearly all those found in Mexican cuisine, but the beverage is subtle and intended to complement, rather than compete with, the dishes it accompanies. And nothing could be more reinvigorating.

The table with the big family has kept Sánchez busy, and now the grandmother, a white-haired woman in a flowered dress, gestures for Sánchez to bring them something from the menu, and the grandfather, smoothing his mustache, calls for more mezcal. Tequila is often thought of as being the ultimate Mexican alcoholic beverage, but tequila is actually just one variety of mezcal, and mezcal, in truth, has a more valid claim on that title.

With a nod, Sánchez zips off to the kitchen to place the family's food order, pan-fried shrimp with potatoes and olives, then returns to place a clean set of tall, narrow glasses on their table beside the requisite saucer of halved limes. Mexican people love their mezcal and tequila, but that doesn't mean they necessarily prefer them unadorned. A sip of straight

*Spiced Holiday Punch
with Guavas and Apples
(page 189), with a
sugarcane stirrer.*

tequila is followed by a lime half covered in sea salt, to be sucked on, so the sour and salty extremity of flavors softens the dramatic taste of alcohol. Follow with another sip of tequila, and repeat.

The lead guitarist of the mariachi troupe takes the young man's request: "Bésame Mucho," that seductive oldie but goodie. As the mariachis begin to croon, the young woman rises and extends her arms in invitation. Delighted, her suitor pushes back his chair, and they begin to dance, causing the children to giggle and shove one another. Sánchez smiles on indulgently. Each of the ten or so waiters at Cantina la Reforma has only a few tables to take care of, and take care of them they do. The atmosphere is familial: show up more than once and you're greeted with an embrace.

In a flourish of strumming, the mariachis wrap up the love song, and the grandparents applaud as the couple returns to their table, flushed and laughing. Sánchez ushers in two new customers, a pair of Dutch travelers on holiday. The fresh-faced young men cheerfully take seats, setting down the cups of tepache they just bought from a vendor on the street. *Tepache* is a traditional, very mildly intoxicating Mexican libation of sun-fermented pineapple rind, water, and piloncillo: fizzy and tangy, almost like ginger ale, with an intriguing nuanced flavor. The mariachis launch into a more rousing number: "*Guantanamera, guajira guantanamera . . .*" It is another old chestnut, and almost everyone in the room who has had a few drinks, and even some who haven't, join in. Even the Dutch travelers, who don't know the words, gamely give it a try, as Sánchez brings them the round of Bohemia beer they've requested.

A cadre of businessmen with loosened ties greet their next round with a cheer. They've ordered *micheladas clásicas*. A jolly beverage for an afternoon out, this preparation is truly Mexican in spirit, making a glass of beer more refreshing by including any of a variety of embellishments, from the simple addition of lime juice to such flourishes as chile powder or tamarind syrup. But what goes into a michelada is really limited only by the drinker's proclivities and imagination and can be so elaborate as to include, for example, Clamato (a tomato juice—clam broth hybrid), mezcal, shrimp powder, and shaved celery, with a head-on shrimp as a garnish. What a way to gild the lily.

Mariachis perform in the Centro Histórico bar La Faena, where complimentary snacks are served to encourage longer stays.

*At the end of an evening at
La Faena, a couple dances
to music on the jukebox.*

A Transplant Turned Native

Beer came late to Mexico: breweries did not arrive in the country until the time of the Industrial Revolution. Once they did, though, it wasn't long before beer became an integral part of Mexican culture. It is a perfect counterpoint to the cuisine's savory, chile-inflected flavors, and in cooking, it enhances broths, marinades, sauces, and stews. Light, refreshing, and well suited to a hot climate, lager is particularly popular. Excellent mainstream brands are Tecate, Victoria, and Pacífico; these vary in color from deep yellow to light amber. Lager makes an ideal chaser for spirits, mellowing the bracing sting of tequila or mezcal (see page 203) and providing a canvas for *micheladas*, beer enriched with lime juice, tomato juice, and other seasonings. Coffee-colored *oscuras*, or dark beers, such as Negra Modelo, have toasted, nutty, and caramel flavors that make them an excellent choice to accompany a richly spiced meal. Mexico only recently began producing stouts (strong-tasting, dark varieties of beer), but unsurprisingly, brewers have showed the national proclivity for bold flavors, the result being that some stouts, such as Házmela Rusa and Lágrimas Negras, have included ingredients like chiles, chocolate, and even coffee. —*Guillermo Ysusi, a Mexico City–based political scientist and beer expert*

Classic Michelada
Michelada Clásica

Michelada refers to beer embellished with condiments such as juice and spices. This is the popular Mexico City cantina version, flavored with a lot of lime juice and served in a salt-rimmed beer stein.

Serves 1

  1 tablespoon flaky sea salt or kosher salt
  1 lime wedge
  1 ounce freshly squeezed lime juice
  One 12-ounce bottle Mexican lager (such as Pacífico) or Vienna lager (such as Negra Modelo), chilled

1 Put the salt onto a flat saucer. Run the lime wedge around the rim of a beer stein to moisten it, then invert the stein and evenly roll the rim in the salt to coat evenly.

2 Add the lime juice to the stein. Pour in the beer, tilting the stein to keep it from foaming over. Stir and serve at once.

Michelada with Mezcal and Lime Juice
Michelada de Camarón

This artful creation (see photograph, page 181), a sort of michelada cocktail based on a recipe by the Mexico City bartender-chef Alex Suástegui, features the tangy combination of Clamato and lime, with the extra kick of tequila or mezcal.

Serves 1

  1 tablespoon flaky sea salt or kosher salt
  ½ teaspoon dried shrimp powder, (available in Mexican shops, or made at home by pulverizing a few dried shrimp in a food processor; optional)
  1 lime wedge
  4 ounces Clamato
  1½ ounces freshly squeezed lime juice

¾ ounce tequila or mezcal

Ice cubes (optional)

One 12-ounce bottle Mexican lager (such as Pacífico) or Vienna lager (such as Negra Modelo), chilled

1 dried head-on shrimp, for garnish (optional)

1 long piece thinly shaved celery stalk, for garnish (optional)

1 Put the salt and ¼ teaspoon of the shrimp powder (if using) onto a flat saucer and mix together. Run the lime wedge around the rim of a large beer stein to moisten it, then invert the stein and evenly roll the rim in the salt mixture to coat evenly.

2 Add the Clamato, lime juice, tequila, the remaining ¼ teaspoon shrimp powder, and a few ice cubes (if using) to the stein and stir briefly to mix. Pour in the beer, tilting the stein to keep it from foaming over. Garnish with the shrimp and celery (if using) and serve at once.

Spiced Holiday Punch with Guavas and Apples
Ponche

This sweet-and-sour holiday punch (see photograph, page 182) is almost a dessert. Any combination of the fruits included here can be used; you can even make it with all apples or all guavas. The tamarind and sugarcane seeds and pith (see page 198) are meant to be discarded after they are chewed for their juice. Adding a splash of tequila or mezcal is known as *ponche con piquete* (punch with a sting).

Serves 4

Two 2½-inch pieces cinnamon stick

3 whole cloves

½ cup pitted prunes

½ cup dried hibiscus flowers (see page 198)

4 whole tamarind pods, peeled and cut into 3-inch pieces (see page 198; optional)

One 8-ounce piloncillo cone (see page 200)

About ½ pound sugarcane, peeled, cut into 3-inch lengths, then sliced lengthwise ¼ inch thick (optional)

10 cups water

4 medium Golden Delicious apples, cut lengthwise into ¼-inch-thick slices

5 medium ripe guavas, ends trimmed, then quartered lengthwise (optional)

1 In a large pot, combine the cinnamon, cloves, prunes, hibiscus, tamarind (if using), piloncillo, sugarcane (if using), and water and bring to a rolling boil over high heat, stirring occasionally. Turn down the heat to medium, cover, and cook at a steady bubble, stirring occasionally, for 45 minutes.

2 Add the apples and guavas (if using), re-cover, and cook, stirring occasionally, until the apples and guavas are very tender, about 30 minutes. Remove punch from the heat and let stand for 15 minutes before serving.

3 Ladle the liquid and fruits into mugs or glasses. Garnish each serving with a piece of sugarcane; it serves as a nifty stirrer.

Chilled Hibiscus Tea with Cinnamon
Agua de Jamaica

An *agua fresca* is a drink made of water infused with fruit or vegetable juices. The word *fresca* suggests a rejuvenating coolness, and also dictates the ideal serving temperature—cool, not cold. A version made with hibiscus is especially popular for its vivid color and tart-sweet flavor.

Serves 4

¾ cup dried hibiscus flowers (see page 198)

1-inch piece cinnamon stick

1 whole clove

½ star anise pod (optional)

6 cups water

¼ cup sugar, plus more if needed

Ice cubes (optional)

1 In a medium saucepan, combine the hibiscus, cinnamon, clove, star anise (if using), and 3 cups of the water and bring to a boil. Turn down the heat to medium and cook at a lively simmer for 5 minutes. Remove from the heat and let steep for 30 minutes.

2 Strain the liquid through a fine-mesh sieve into a pitcher. Add the remaining 3 cups water and the sugar and stir until the sugar is fully dissolved. Taste for sweetness, adding more sugar if desired. Serve in tall glasses, over ice if you like.

Cucumber, Celery, and Mint Juice
Agua de Pepino, Apio, y Menta

The fresh taste of cucumber and celery in this agua fresca, with the addition of mint and lime juice, is wonderfully quenching on a hot day.

Serves 4
    6 cups water
    ¾ cup sugar
    2 tablespoons freshly squeezed lime juice
    1 celery stalk, coarsely chopped
    1 cup coarsely chopped cucumber
        (preferably Kirby)
    10 fresh peppermint leaves
    Ice cubes (optional)

1 In a blender, combine the water, sugar, lime juice, celery, cucumber, and mint and blend until very smooth (you can strain the liquid through a fine-mesh sieve, but it is unnecessary).

2 Transfer to a pitcher and serve in tall glasses, over ice if you like.

Mexican-Style Spiced Coffee
Café de Olla

The scent of *café de olla*—coffee brewed with piloncillo, spices like cloves and cinnamon, and orange peel—is a signature aroma of the Mexico City morning. The seasonings can be adjusted to taste, and if you don't like your coffee sweet, just leave out the piloncillo.

Makes 9 cups
    One 8-ounce piloncillo cone (see page 200)
    2 whole cloves
    Peel of 1 orange, cut into 2-inch pieces
    Two 2½-inch pieces cinnamon stick
    9 cups water
    1 cup medium- or coarse-grind
        medium-roast coffee

In a large pot, combine the piloncillo, cloves, orange peel, cinnamon, and water and bring to boil, stirring occasionally. Turn down the heat to medium-low and continue to simmer, stirring occasionally, for 7 minutes. Add the coffee and simmer for 5 minutes. Remove from the heat and let stand for 2 minutes. Strain through a fine-mesh sieve into a coffee pot or pitcher and serve at once.

Sangrita

Sweet, sour, spicy, and delicious, this heady beverage is a traditional accompaniment to tequila shots.

Makes about 1½ cups
    1 cup canned tomato juice
    ½ cup freshly squeezed orange juice
    1 tablespoon freshly squeezed lime juice
    1 tablespoon Worcestershire sauce
    1 teaspoon Tabasco sauce
    1 tablespoon sugar
    ½ teaspoon salt

1 In a pitcher, combine all of the ingredients and stir until the sugar and salt are fully dissolved. Let stand for 15 minutes.

2 Stir again briefly, then serve in shot glasses as a chaser for tequila.

Mexico City Referencia

General Notes on Ingredients

To cook food that tastes authentically Mexican, use the freshest ingredients possible. Try to buy locally produced fruits and vegetables, dairy products, and meat and poultry at farmers' markets and farms or through CSAs in your area. Talk with the vendors, as they might carry items you wouldn't expect, or they might know of a nearby dairy that, for example, makes Mexican cheeses. Think creatively: perhaps your neighbors sell fresh eggs or surplus zucchini from their garden, or maybe you grow fresh mint. Alternatively, try natural foods markets, both small stores and chains like Whole Foods. Another place to look for ingredients are the chains that specialize in Mexican and Central American products, such as Vallarta Supermarkets in southern California or Supremo Food Markets in the Northeast. These carry the relevant products, such as the thick, lightly soured cream called *crema* and the cones of unrefined sugar known as *piloncillo*. But these days, even general markets tend to carry Mexican items beyond taco shells and salsa. Be on the lookout for what's available—and

be open to inspiration. For example, you might notice that next to the usual Tabasco sauce is the can of chipotles en adobo called for in Flank Steak and Avocado Tostadas (page 32). Read the labels: your rule of thumb, from bacon to tortillas and everything in between, is to look for the furthest-away expiry date and the fewest ingredients.

Avocado If you live in a region where avocados are grown, look for varieties that aren't sold in supermarkets, such as the Fuerte, which has smooth, dark green skin. Otherwise, the Hass variety, which is squat and has bumpy dark green to black skin, is a good choice. Select a plump, firm fruit that feels heavy for its size and shows no signs of brittleness or shrinkage. When using avocado in any of these recipes, it must be ripe: if you press gently around the stem, it should yield slightly. To hasten ripening, leave an avocado inside a paper bag, unrefrigerated, for a day or so. Once ripe, use quickly. It's best to keep the fruits unrefrigerated, even when making guacamole. If you must store leftovers, place in a sealable bag and refrigerate. Before eating, scrape off the browned surface. A partially eaten avocado will generally keep for a day or two.

Beans and Legumes You can find most of the dried beans and legumes called for in this book—black, pinto, Great Northern, lentils—at any supermarket. Online vendors, such as Ranchogordo.com, who source from small-batch farmers, tend to have excellent products on offer. Hundreds of bean varieties are available, and you're encouraged to experiment. Always rinse beans thoroughly, even if the label says "pre-washed," and watch for pebbles. Store in tightly capped glass containers and keep in a cool, dark place for up to 6 months.

Fava Yellowish and with an irregular ovoid shape, dried peeled fava beans have a distinctive sharp taste that pairs well with masa-based recipes. Look for them in Middle Eastern or Latin markets, and read the labeling carefully to be sure you are buying peeled favas.

Lentil The lentils used in Mexican cooking tend to be brown and very small, similar in size to the Puy green lentils of France, and have a lively, peppery flavor. The more commonly found larger brown lentils are a fine substitution, though they will require a longer cooking time than suggested in the recipes in this book. Lentils can dry out quickly as they cook, so keep a close eye on them as they cook to be sure there's enough liquid in the pot.

Peruano Also known as Mexican yellow beans, these medium-size oval, pale yellow beans are popular throughout Mexico for their creamy texture and mild flavor. Great Northern beans are a good substitute.

Mexican-Style Stewed Beans
Frijoles de la Olla

While this can be eaten just as it is, this is also the master recipe for the beans that get used in many other dishes in this book, such Guadalajara-Style Beef and Bean Stew (page 147). There's no hard-and-fast rule to their cooking time; it depends entirely on the type of bean used, taking anywhere from around 2 hours to more than twice that. Some say that soaking the beans overnight in room-temperature water reduces the cooking time by about half, though that hasn't been proven. Freshness is also a factor in cooking time: the fresher the beans, the shorter the cooking time. This recipe will yield enough cooked beans for any of the dishes in this book, plus some extra that can be stored in an airtight container in the refrigerator for up to 1 week.

Note that you don't add salt to the beans until they are cooked.

Makes about 5 cups

2½ cups dried beans (such as black, pinto, Great Northern, or peruano), rinsed
5 cups water
½ medium white onion, halved
4 garlic cloves
3 epazote sprigs (see page 198; optional)
Salt

1 In a medium pot, combine the beans, water, onion, and garlic and bring to a boil over high heat, skimming off any foam that forms on the surface. Turn down the heat to medium-low, cover partially, and continue to cook, stirring occasionally, until the beans are soft and tender but retain their shape, 2½ to 4½ hours, depending on the bean and its freshness. The beans should always be covered by at least ½ inch water, so every 15 minutes or so, check the water level, adding ½ to 1 cup more hot water as needed.

2 When the beans are ready, with the back of a large spoon, spend a minute or two smashing some of the beans against the bottom of the pot. By breaking up some of the beans up, you're creating a thicker sauce, and if you mash some of the garlic or onion, the result will be even better. At this point, at least ¼ inch of liquid should be covering the beans; if they look too dry, add hot water as needed to reach the needed level. Add the epazote (if using) and 1 tablespoon salt, raise the heat to medium, and cook, stirring occasionally, for a minute or two (this is an important step to get an accurate sense of saltiness). Taste again and add more salt if needed, then use right away or store until needed.

Fava Bean Variation: For the Fava Bean–Stuffed Masa Cakes on page 68, you will need 1 cup mashed fava beans seasoned with mint. Follow the directions for stewed beans, using ¾ cup dried peeled fava beans (see left) for the beans, reducing the onion and garlic by half, and omitting the epazote. Combine the favas, onion, garlic, a sprig of spearmint or peppermint, and water to cover generously in a medium pot and cook as directed. Then, using the back of a large spoon, mash the beans, onion, garlic, mint, and the beans' remaining cooking liquid in the pot; this should yield about 1½ cups of mashed fava beans. Add salt to taste. Eat leftovers as a dip with Tortilla Chips (page 201).

Refried Beans
Frijoles Refritos

These beans are called for in Tamales Stuffed with Refried Beans (page 62), or you can eat them as is, with some Cotija cheese (see right) crumbled on top, as a complement to nearly any savory dish in this book.

Makes about 2½ cups
- 1 heaping tablespoon pork lard or canola oil
- ¼ medium white onion, minced
- 1 garlic clove, minced
- 2½ cups cooked black beans with their cooking liquid (see left)
- 1 dried avocado leaf (see page 198), finely crumbled (optional)
- Salt

1 In a 12-inch skillet, heat the lard over medium-low heat. Add the onion and cook, stirring often, until translucent, about 5 minutes. Add the garlic and cook, stirring often, until the garlic has softened and the onion is just turning golden, about 4 minutes longer.

2 Add the beans and their liquid and the avocado leaves (if using) and, using a masher or the bottom of a glass, mash all of the beans into the onion and fat until you have a paste the consistency of chunky peanut butter, about 10 minutes. If the mixture begins to dry out too much as you work, add more cooking liquid from the beans or warm water, ¼ cup at a time. Season to taste with salt.

Canola Oil This pale yellow oil has a high smoking point and mild flavor, which allows strong seasoning to shine through. Sunflower, safflower, peanut, and grapeseed oil are good substitutions. Store oil in a glass container in a cool, dark place. Always make sure your oil is fresh, which is discernible by a clean, appealing aroma. If you would like to experiment with traditional Mexican cooking fat, use melted pork lard (see page 199) in place of canola oil in the savory recipes that call for sautéeing.

Carnitas A classic of the state of Michoacán, *carnitas* is pork cooked in pork lard for hours and usually seasoned with garlic, thyme, oregano, and bay leaves. It is served most frequently as a stuffing for tacos, but it is also used in sandwiches (page 139) or as an excellent main course. You may be able to buy it by the pound from a restaurant or taco truck specializing in it, but making your own, though the dish requires a large quantity of lard, is not difficult. The carnitas will keep in an airtight container in the refrigerator for up to 1 week. The leftover lard will keep frozen for up to 6 months.

Mexican-Style Pork Confit
Carnitas

Makes about 1¼ pounds or 3½ cups
- 3 pounds pork lard
- 1 pound boneless pork leg, cut into 4-inch chunks
- 1 pound baby-back pork ribs (about 8 ribs), cut in half
- ½ medium white onion
- 8 garlic cloves
- 3 thyme sprigs, or ¼ teaspoon dried thyme
- 3 oregano sprigs, or ¼ teaspoon dried oregano
- 5 bay leaves
- Salt

1 In a Dutch oven or other large, heavy pot, melt the lard over medium heat. Add both meats, the onion, garlic, thyme, oregano, bay leaves, and 1 tablespoon salt and stir to combine; the melted lard should cover the meat and, as it becomes hotter, bubble up around it. Turn down the heat as low as possible and cook the meat, stirring occasionally, until golden and very tender, about 2 hours. Monitor the heat closely, as you want a very gentle simmer, with the fat at a lazy bubble. If the meat is not ready yet, cook for up to 30 minutes longer.

2 Remove from the heat, then remove the meat from the lard. When it is cool enough to handle, shred the meat, following the grain, with two forks, discarding the bones, then cut into bite-size pieces if making sandwiches or as desired for other uses. Taste for salt.

Cheeses Authentic Mexican cheeses might be difficult to find in your area, so some suggested substitutions are included here. But you are encouraged to experiment and use your instincts about what cheese most appeals to you.
  Cotija ① A variety of *queso añejo* (a general Mexican term for aged hard cheese), Cotija is used in the recipes that call for an aged cheese; *cincho*, pictured on the next page, is a similar variety from Guerrero state. Cotija cheese crumbled with the tines of a fork helps transform recipes into complex and robust dishes. If you can't find Cotija, try a good Pecorino Romano, coarsely grated with the tines of a fork.

Ranchero ② is a classic Mexican melting or table cheese that resembles a mild feta in taste, though it is made with cow's milk.

Manchego ③ A Mexican variation on the classic Spanish cheese of the same name, Manchego is sharp and Cheddar-like and tends to melt very well. Good-quality, medium- to extra-sharp, genuine Cheddar makes a good substitute. The variety of Manchego shown has been flavored with fresh, ripe jalapeño chiles and fresh epazote.

Quesillo ④ Also known as queso Oaxaca, this excellent melting cheese, usually in the shape of a ball, hails, as the name suggests, from the state of Oaxaca. String cheese is a fine substitute.

Panela ⑤ is a fresh cow's-milk cheese that is Mexico's answer to mozzarella, which can be substituted.

Chicharrón Pork rind fried in pork lard, *chicharrón* is a salty and addictive treat. At Mexican or Central American butchers, you can buy chicharrón by the ounce in single large sheets roughly the size of a pizza. Barring that, ordinary fried pork rind is available wherever groceries are sold. Chicharrón will keep, tightly wrapped and refrigerated, for up to 2 weeks.

Chicken Buy chicken labeled organic and free-range from a butcher or grocery store. While you can use precut chicken parts, dishes will taste significantly better if you start with a small whole fryer or roaster; use the equivalent weight of the pieces called for in the recipes. For Green Mole with Chicken (page 147) or Milpa Alta Chicken Mole (page 138), you can use a whole chicken cut into ten or sixteen pieces. Cut up the chicken yourself or ask your butcher to cut it into pieces, specifying the number. Be vigilant about freshness, and try to avoid frozen chicken altogether. Look for flesh that is plump and full, with moist, clear skin that gives off little aroma. Many of the recipes in this book also call for homemade chicken broth, and two recipes call for shredded chicken breast. You can use dark meat for the shredded chicken, but you'll get a more traditional result by using the breast.

Mexican Chicken Broth
Consomé de Pollo

This broth is called for in numerous recipes in this book. Using a whole cut-up chicken, it can also be made into *caldo de pollo*, a substantial stew, with the addition of another cilantro sprig or two, a couple of spearmint or peppermint sprigs, a few peeled carrots cut into thick coins, and a chayote

(see page 203) or two, peeled and cut into thick chunks. When the chicken is cooked, rather than straining the broth, serve it as is along with the chicken pieces and garnish it with minced jalapeño or serrano chile, minced white onion, and chopped cilantro and plenty of limes for squeezing on top. Note, however, that the two versions—broth and stew—are not interchangeable. Recipes calling for chicken broth require the following preparation.

Makes about 5 cups

- 2½ pounds bone-in, skin-on chicken parts (preferably dark meat)
- 1 medium white onion, quartered
- 5 garlic cloves
- Salt
- 2 bay leaves
- 3 whole allspice berries
- 4 cilantro sprigs

1 In a large pot, combine the chicken, onion, garlic, and 2 teaspoons salt. Add cold water to cover by about 1 inch (about 7 cups), stir well, and bring to a boil. Turn down the heat to medium-low; you want to maintain a good, steady simmer for the duration of the cooking. Skim off and discard any foam that forms, then stir in the bay leaves, allspice, and cilantro. Cook uncovered at a steady

simmer, stirring occasionally and periodically skimming off the fat if desired, until you have a richly flavorful broth, about 1½ hours.

2 Remove from the heat, then taste for salt and add more if needed. Scoop out the chicken pieces and discard or use for another purpose. Strain the stock through a fine-mesh sieve and discard any solids. The broth can be used right away or stored. To store, let cool, cover, and refrigerate for up to 5 days or freeze for up to a few months.

Shredded Poached Chicken Breast
Pollo Desmenuzado

Makes about 2 cups

> 1 bone-in, skin-on chicken breast (about 1 pound)
> ½ medium white onion
> 3 garlic cloves
> 8 whole allspice berries
> 2 bay leaves
> Salt

1 In a medium saucepan, combine the chicken, onion, garlic, allspice, bay leaves, 1 teaspoon salt, and water to cover by about 1 inch. Bring to a simmer, cover partially, and cook at a simmer, monitoring the heat to be sure the liquid doesn't boil, until the chicken is cooked through but still juicy, 35 to 40 minutes. To test for doneness, pierce the chicken with a fork; if the juices run clear, it's ready.

2 Scoop out the chicken and set aside to cool. If the cooking liquid is called for in a recipe, strain it and set it aside; if not, strain it and reserve it for another use or discard. When the chicken is cool enough to handle, shred it very finely using your fingers, following the grain and discarding all the bones, skin, and sinew. Sprinkle to taste with salt. Use right away, or store in an airtight container in the refrigerator for up to a few days.

Chiles For a detailed guide to the varieties and their flavor profiles called for in the recipes, see pages 128 to 131.

Fresh Chiles When buying serrano, jalapeño, poblano, habanero, árbol, or other fresh chiles, look for bright, taut, shiny, glistening skin and a fresh-looking stem and, generally speaking, choose the smallest specimens available. Store fresh chiles in the refrigerator in a plastic bag for up to a week or so, keeping them as dry as possible.

To stem and seed a fresh chile, the best implements are a paring knife and a plastic cutting board. Use latex gloves if you're concerned about capsaicin—the active element in chiles—irritating your skin. Lop off the stem and cut the chile in half lengthwise. With the knife, scrape out all the interior matter (seeds and pith) and discard it immediately. After handling the chile, wash your hands, the cutting board, and the knife thoroughly with plenty of warm, soapy water.

Dried Chiles The most commonly used dried chiles—ancho, árbol, pasilla, guajillo, pulla, and mulato—are easily found prepackaged in many supermarkets. In large Mexican grocery stores, they're typically sold in bulk, usually in the produce section. Look for chiles that exhibit signs of freshness—flexible, light sheen, slightly fruity aroma—passing up any that are brittle, dusty, or appear faded. Store them in tightly sealed containers in a cool, dark place for up to 1 year.

The best implement to use to stem and seed a dried chile is either a paring knife or kitchen shears. As with fresh chiles, don latex gloves if you're concerned about irritating your skin. Rinse the chile and pat it dry. Cut off the stem, then split the chile lengthwise. Splay it open and tap out the seeds, discarding them immediately. After handling the chile, wash your hands, the cutting board, and the knife or shears with warm, soapy water.

When pan-toasting a dried chile, make sure you pull it from the heat as soon as it is fragrant; you don't want it to be smoking or burned. When soaking dried chiles, submerge them in very hot water until they are soft and pliable.

Bottled Chile Sauce Called "hot sauce" in the United States, this is such a cherished condiment in Mexico City that any snack, from thick-sliced jicama to *totopos*, hardly qualifies as such without a splash on top. Hot sauce is even added to beer. Look for Salsa Valentina, in a squat glass bottle; the yellow label indicates ordinary heat, the black label signifies a fierier brew. Tapatío is another delicious brand.

Canned Chipotle Chiles Also known as *chipotles en adobo*, these are smoke-dried whole jalapeño chiles that have been cooked in a tomato-based sauce. Any brand makes a delicious addition to salsas and many other dishes; try tucking a canned chile into plain Cheese Quesadillas (page 61) for a real treat. They are found in many supermarkets stocked alongside other canned Mexican foods. Store the unused portion refrigerated in a glass jar.

Chiles Güeros Encurtidos Pale yellow and varying in heat from mild to medium hot, these canned or jarred chiles are cured along with carrots and onions in a vinegar brine. They are available in Mexican markets, but pickled Italian peppers (pepperoncini) are an acceptable substitute.

Roasting Poblano Chiles To roast a poblano, put the whole chile directly on the flame of a gas burner for a few minutes, turning it until the surface blisters and darkens on all sides as completely as possible. Wrap tightly in a kitchen towel or enclose in a plastic bag for 5 minutes. Then, with a spoon or paring knife, scrape off the skin. Cut the chile open and remove and discard seeds and pith, then rinse and pat the chile dry with a paper towel and sprinkle the inside with a little salt. If you do not have a gas range, an electric burner or a broiler can be used.

Chorizo This fresh, Mexicanized version of the traditional Spanish pork sausage gets its intense flavor from cumin and garlic and its deep red color from guajillo chiles. It is sold in round links about the size of a golf ball; discard the casing before using. Look for it at Mexican or Central American grocery stores. Mexican chorizo will keep well wrapped in the refrigerator for up to one week. Fry leftover Mexican chorizo and scramble into eggs for breakfast.

Corn Tortillas These flat, round breads are the jewels in the crown of the Mexican table. In this book, only corn tortillas are called for, though other types, such as flour tortillas, could be substituted. The best option is to make tortillas yourself using the recipe that follows or to visit a tortilla manufacturer that sells them retail. Other good bets include Whole Foods, local specialty foods markets, and Mexican grocers. As always, freshness and a lack of additives are key: the best tortillas are made of only corn, water, and *cal* (calcium hydroxide). There are delicious varieties available made of purple corn; light-green-colored tortillas are corn masa flavored with ground nopales. In supermarkets, check the refrigerated section first, as tortillas kept on open shelves tend to have preservatives. Store purchased or homemade tortillas tightly wrapped in plastic in the refrigerator for no longer than 1 week.

To heat tortillas, place them onto a hot skillet or comal over medium heat until they are hot and supple, about 30 seconds on each side. Or, using tongs, heat each tortilla directly over a medium-low gas flame, flipping it until both sides pick up a few black spots. Tortillas cool down quickly, so if heating many at a time, wrap them in a kitchen towel or put them into a tortillero (see page 198) until serving.

To accompany a meal, a good flour tortilla can be just as delicious. Versions are available in nearly every market, but, again, try to find those without additives, made with only flour, salt, and shortening (traditionally lard). Store and heat as you would a corn tortilla.

Homemade Corn Tortillas

For instructions on how to pat tortillas out by hand, see the sidebar on page 62. For this recipe, you'll need a tortilla press.

Makes about sixteen 6-inch tortillas

    3 cups Fresh Homemade Masa (about 1½ pounds; page 199) or store-bought

1 Have ready a tortilla press and a medium bowl full of water. Portion the masa into 16 small balls of about 2 tablespoons each. Cover them with a clean, damp kitchen towel. Cut a large ziplock or clean plastic grocery bag into two 7-inch squares. Place one of the squares onto the lower plate of the tortilla press.

2 Heat a comal or a 12-inch skillet over medium heat. Moisten your hands in the bowl of water. Pick up a ball of masa and, using your moistened hands, flatten it into a disk about 3 inches in diameter and ⅓ inch thick, then smooth out the edges. Place the disk in the center of the plastic-topped lower plate of the press, then lay the second square of plastic on top of it. Firmly close the press to flatten the tortilla. Lift the top of the press, rotate the tortilla 180 degrees, and firmly close the press again. The tortilla should be round and about ¹⁄₁₆ inch thick at this point.

3 Lift the tortilla from the press with the bottom plastic sheet, flip the tortilla over onto your outstretched hand, and peel away the plastic. Carefully slide the tortilla onto the hot pan and cook until the top looks slightly dry and the bottom releases easily from the pan, about 30 seconds. Flip the tortilla over and cook for about 1 minute; the top should puff up and the bottom will pick up a few toasty golden spots. If serving right away, transfer the cooked tortilla to a clean kitchen towel and fold the towel over to cover, or transfer it to a towel-lined tortillero. Cook the remaining tortillas the same way, stacking them inside the folded towel or the tortillero so they stay warm and soft until serving.

Crema Cow's milk cream that has been fermented and has the consistency of yogurt with a faintly tart taste, *crema* is typically drizzled on top of dishes

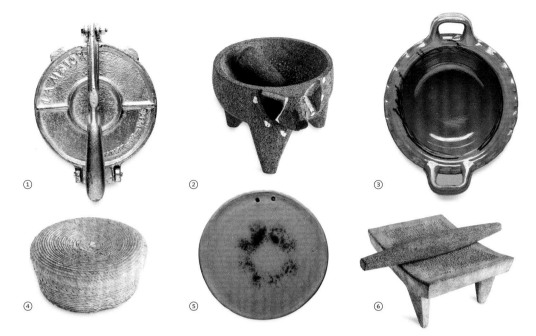

① ② ③
④ ⑤ ⑥

as a garnish. In markets, you'll find commercially made crema of different regional and national varieties. If you find one that doesn't have many additives, use that; otherwise, you can substitute a quality sour cream thinned with a tiny bit of water to the consistency of a thin milkshake. Crema keeps refrigerated for 2 to 3 weeks.

Equipment To make the recipes in this book, you don't need much in the way of specific equipment, barring a couple of those listed below (and if you don't have them, you can improvise). However, just a few pieces of inexpensive Mexican cookware will yield great results. These can be found at shops that carry Mexican wares and at online retailers.

Blender Mexican foods that require grinding are traditionally made in a molcajete (see below), but a blender works fine. Use it methodically, as though you were grinding by hand, by putting it on a low speed and pulsing the ingredients.

Cazuela ③ A large clay pot, the *cazuela* is particularly suited for simmering stews, such as the Mexican-Style Stewed Zucchini and Poblanos on page 90.

Comal ⑤ A round grill ranging in size from 1 to 3 feet in diameter, the comal is designed to sit directly atop the heat source. The genius of the comal is in its even heat distribution. The best are made of clay (as shown), cast iron, or carbon steel.

Fine-Mesh Sieve Look for sturdy models with handles made of heatproof rubber or metal; avoid plastic sieves.

Flanera Called for in Flan (page 174), this pan, sometimes available with a nonstick coating, resembles a cake pan the size of a standard spring-form but with a clamp-on lid; the desired *flanera*

size is 7 inches in diameter. The flan is assembled in the *flanera*, then the *flanera* is placed inside a larger pot to which a couple of inches of water has been added, creating a water bath, also known as a bain-marie, for slow, even cooking. A 6- or 8-inch cake pan tightly covered with aluminum foil can be substituted.

Metate ⑥ This two-part implement has been used in the Mesoamerican kitchen since ancient times for grinding nixtamalized corn into masa.

Molcajete ② Nothing is better for making salsa and grinding spices than this three-legged mortar with a large bowl and its accompanying pestle, or *tejolote*. The best molcajetes are made of basalt (volcanic stone); the rough texture assists in the grinding process. For the recipes in this book, a molcajete that is at least 10 inches in diameter is ideal.

Olla A large bulbous-shaped traditional clay pot with handles and a lid, an *olla* cooks beans in less than the usual time, thanks to its distinctive design.

Tamalera A pot specially designed for steaming tamales, the *tamalera* includes a built-in perforated rack for holding the tamales safely above the steaming water.

Tortilla Press ① Tortilla presses, or *tortilladoras*, vary in quality depending on the brand. They come in a variety of materials, from aluminum to wood, with heavy metal the most common, and typically range in size from 6 to 8 inches across. A 6-inch press was used for the recipe for Homemade Corn Tortillas on page 196. Using a press will ensure your tortillas come out uniform, and it is a fun tool to have. Patting tortillas out by hand is, however, a time-honored method; see page 62 for instructions.

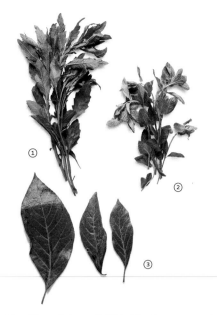

①

②

③

Tortillero ④ A small lidded basket or container, a *tortillero* is used for storing and serving hot tortillas, which otherwise dry out and cool down quickly.

Fruits All of the fruits called for in this book are generally available wherever tropical produce is sold. Asian, Caribbean, African, and Latin American shops or supermarkets are good sources.

Guava Round and with edible shiny skin and small seeds, guavas have a sunny sweetness and a clean, sharp aroma. The variety eaten in Mexico is yellow and a bit larger than a golf ball. Other types—in different sizes and colors—are available in Asian markets. No matter what variety you choose, check for ripeness: it should yield slightly when pressed. Store at room temperature.

Lime The sharp, clean taste of fresh lime squeezed over a dish just before it's eaten is an essential flavor component of Mexico City food. Any type will work, but Key limes are the most authentic. Choose fruits that are plump and heavy for their size and with no signs of wrinkling or bruising. Limes will keep for a week or so refrigerated and for a few days unrefrigerated.

Pineapple Look for smaller fruits that are heavy for their size and are firm, yellow, and fragrant. Try to pull a leaf from near the center of the crown: if one comes out easily, the pineapple is ripe. You can also ripen it at home at room temperature. Once it has been cut, store it well wrapped in the refrigerator.

Plantain While it looks like a large banana, the flesh inside is much denser and less sweet. Look for very ripe ones, which have yellow skin heavily mottled with black. You can eat a ripe plantain as you would a regular banana. Store at room temperature.

Sugarcane Resembling stout green bamboo canes, sugarcane is very hard, jointed, and fibrous, so

if you select a long one, you will need to use a cleaver to peel it and cut it into more manageable lengths, or you can ask the vendor to possibly cut it for you.

Tamarind A cocoa-brown seedpod with sticky flesh and a tart flavor, whole tamarind pods come fresh in produce sections or in packages, usually with the (inedible) shells and seeds present. To peel, press against the exterior with the palm of your hand and remove the shell. Store unused portions in an airtight container in a cool, dark place for up to 1 year.

Herbs Fresh herbs are best when they are home-grown or have been bought from a farmers' market or farm stand. Use fresh herbs as soon as possible and store them refrigerated in a plastic bag along with a paper towel; store dried herbs in glass jars in a cool, dark place for up to a few months.

Avocado Leaf ③ Glossy and dark green when fresh and a matte pale green when dry, avocado leaves have a subtle anise-like scent. They are used whole or crumbled. Look for them in Mexican grocery stores where the herbs and spices are kept.

Bay Leaf An aromatic addition to soups, sauces, and marinades, bay leaves can be used fresh or dried in equal quantity. Dried bay leaves are called for in these recipes, but if you can find fresh ones, use them—they have a more dynamic flavor.

Epazote ① Resembling dandelion greens in appearance, epazote has a fresh, distinctive flavor that resembles menthol. The leaves should be bright green and not droopy. Dried epazote is an ineffective substitute.

Hibiscus This deep wine-red dried flower lends tartness to beverages. Note that while in natural foods stores and herb shops the flower is labeled as hibiscus, in Mexican markets, it will be labeled *flor de jamaica.*

Oregano, Dried Look for Mexican oregano (check the product's label for country of origin), which has a sharp, concentrated, earthy taste. Barring that, use regular (Mediterranean) oregano.

Spearmint ② Also known as *yerba buena* or *hierbabuena*, spearmint has a clean, refined flavor. It looks like peppermint, though with paler green leaves. If you cannot find it, peppermint is a fine substitute. Absent fresh mint of either variety, it's better to leave it out of the recipe than to use dried mint, which has a different flavor.

Hominy Not to be confused with hominy grits, the hominy called for in Slow-Cooked Pork and Hominy Stew (page 58) comes in a can. It's maize that has been briefly cooked with water and a small quantity of calcium hydroxide in order to soften it and improve its nutritive value. For the pozole recipe, use a 105-ounce can, drained.

Masa Made from dried corn that has been cooked with an alkaline solution, rested overnight, washed thoroughly several times, and then ground into a dough, masa is one of the fundamental ingredients of Mexican cooking. It is made into myriad forms, notably tortillas, and can be steamed, shaped, deep-fried, grilled, and used as a thickener for beverages. If you live in a place where there is a tortilla manufacturer or a Mexican supermarket, the easiest option is to buy prepared masa by the pound there. You can also buy dried ground masa, known as masa harina or corn flour, and prepare it as instructed in the accompanying recipe. Masa harina labeled "organic" or "non-GMO," such as Bob's Red Mill brand (available in supermarkets and online), should be your first choice. Otherwise, the most commonly found brand is Maseca. Look for it in the flour section, in bags that mirror the size of all-purpose flour bags. Masa is made from white corn, yellow corn, or blue corn; each has marginally different flavor characteristics, but they are largely uniform in their properties. Store dried masa as you would flour, in a cool, dark place.

Fresh Homemade Masa
Masa Fresca

Makes 3 cups (1½ pounds)
    3 cups dried, ground masa harina
    Salt
    1¼ cups warm water

In a large bowl, mix together the masa harina and ½ teaspoon salt. While continuously mixing with your hands or a spoon, gradually add the water in a slow, steady stream. Then knead the masa until you have a large smooth ball. It should be slightly tacky to the touch and the edges should not crack easily when a small ball of it is pressed flat between your palms. It may be necessary to knead in a little more water, 1 tablespoon at a time, to reach the proper consistency. Taste for salt and add more if needed. Use the dough as soon as possible.

Octopus If you buy a fresh, whole octopus for Braised Octopus with Garlic and Guajillo Chiles (page 110), look for one that's between 3 and 4 pounds. If possible, ask the fishmonger to clean it for you. To clean it yourself, first rinse it under cold running water. Locate the head—the bulbous sac atop the legs—and remove and discard the gelatinous substance inside. Flip the octopus over and locate the hard beak at the very center of its underside. With a sharp paring knife, insert the blade about 1 inch deep and, working in a circular motion, remove and discard all of the hard, tough matter, including the beak. Rinse the octopus again before cooking. If you have purchased a frozen octopus, which is typically sold already cleaned, let it thaw in the refrigerator overnight, then rinse before cooking. If it has not thawed completely by the time you are ready to cook, run cold water on it to help it along.

Parboiled Rice Called for in Paella Mexicana (page 108), parboiled rice is rice that is steam-pressured before it is hulled, resulting in grains that retain their integrity after cooking. It can be found in bulk where Indian ingredients are sold or in packages in many supermarkets, usually under the Carolina or Golden Canilla (Goya) brand. Uncle Ben's "converted" rice is another term for the same product.

Pepitas Oval green Mexican pumpkin seeds with a nutty texture and flavor, shelled *pepitas* are called for in Green Mole with Chicken (page 147). Regular jack-o'-lantern pumpkin seeds are not an acceptable substitute. You can find pepitas at Mexican grocery stores. For mole verde, use raw, not roasted, pepitas.

Pork Lard The traditional cooking fat of Mexico, pork lard can be used for frying in many of the savory recipes in this book and is essential for making carnitas (page 139) and some of the masa recipes (with apologies to vegetarians, solid vegetable shortening is not a good substitute). Lard should be creamy beige and have a mild, porky aroma. Ask a butcher to sell you some. Otherwise, Armor is the most widely available brand; in addition to being labeled "lard," it will likely be marked *manteca* ("lard" in Spanish). Stored in plastic wrap or in an airtight container in the coldest part of the refrigerator, it will last for up to 3 weeks, or it can be kept frozen for up to 6 months.

Pickles Vegetables that have been cured, usually in a spicy brine like the Pickled Chiles and Vegetables with Thyme, Oregano, and Bay Leaves on page 38, are an extremely popular Mexican table condiment. Here's a quick no-cook recipe that can be prepared in minutes. It can be eaten with virtually any savory dish in the book.

Pickled Red Onions
Cebollas Moradas en Escabeche

Makes about 1 cup
    1 red onion, thinly sliced lengthwise
    ¼ cup freshly squeezed lime juice
    Salt
    Pinch of dried oregano (optional)

1 Put the onion slices in a small nonreactive bowl and stir in the lime juice, a couple of hefty pinches of salt, and the oregano (if using). Let marinate for at least 30 minutes, stirring occasionally.

2 The onions can be served right away. Store any leftovers in an airtight container in the refrigerator for up to 3 days.

Piloncillo Made of sugarcane juice boiled down into cone-shaped blocks and hardened, *piloncillo* is rock hard, deep golden, and tastes earthy. There are numerous varieties available in Mexican markets, and as a general rule of thumb, the price will reflect the quality. The cones also come in various sizes, from 4 ounces up to half a pound. The piloncillo cones used in the recipes in this book weigh about 8 ounces. If you can only find cones of another size, adjust the amount of piloncillo you use according to weight. While brown sugar is the closest corollary to the flavor of piloncillo, it does not make a suitable substitute.

Salsas You won't find a salt shaker on the Mexican dining table. Salsa is the staple seasoning, providing both saltiness and zest to foods. There are literally thousands of varieties with umpteen regional variations, from the raw salsa on the southwest coast that calls for dried whole small shrimp to the salsas of Central Mexico, in which all of the ingredients are grilled on a comal—and all of them can be found in Mexico City. In bringing together the many fundamental cooking techniques of Mexico, salsa embodies aspects of the cuisine that can be endlessly expanded upon—and makes virtually everything taste better. The two salsa recipes that follow are excellent companions to most of the savory dishes in this book. The Mexican tomato sauce serves as the gravy component of Ancho Chiles Stuffed with Manchego Cheese (page 89). All three recipes can truly be called essentials.

Grilled Tomato and Green Chile Salsa
Salsa Roja

Among the many varieties of salsa, *salsa roja* (shown opposite, right) reigns supreme. The secret to its flavor comes from grilling the tomatoes, onion, garlic, and chiles until they pick up char marks on their surface. However, a no-cook cousin to this salsa (*salsa cruda*, known in the United States as *pico de gallo*) can easily be made. Simply omit the garlic, mince all of the other ingredients instead of grinding them, and stir to mix.

Makes about 1½ cups

> 3 medium Roma tomatoes
> ½ small white onion, quartered and separated into individual layers
> 3 garlic cloves, unpeeled
> 1 to 5 serrano chiles, depending on the amount of heat desired
> ½ cup loosely packed fresh cilantro leaves plus about 2 inches of their stems, coarsely chopped
> Salt

1 Heat a comal or a 12-inch skillet over medium-high heat. When the pan is hot, place the tomatoes, onion, garlic, and chile(s) onto the pan and grill, turning them with tongs just once or twice on each side, until all of the ingredients have picked up some charred spots, 10 to 20 minutes, depending on the vegetable. As the tomatoes and onion are ready, transfer them to a blender. As the chile(s) and garlic are ready, transfer them to a plate.

2 Stem the chile(s) and peel the garlic, then add them to the blender along with the cilantro and ½ teaspoon salt. Grind the ingredients, pulsing two or three times or more, until the salsa is the consistency you prefer, whether coarse, smooth, or somewhere in between. Taste for salt and add more if needed. If the salsa is too thick, add water, a couple of teaspoons at a time, to achieve a thinner consistency. You can instead use a molcajete (see page 197) to grind the salsa: start by adding some salt, the onion and garlic, then the chile(s) and cilantro, and finally the tomatoes, grinding after the addition of each ingredient until it is the consistency you prefer.

3 Serve at once, or store in a glass jar in the refrigerator for up to 5 days.

Tomatillo Salsa
Salsa Verde

This is a tart green corollary to salsa roja made with tomatillos and serrano chiles. An alternative is to skip grilling the ingredients and instead just grind them raw (peel the garlic) in a blender or molcajete.

Makes about ¾ cup
 5 medium tomatillos, husks removed and rinsed
 1 or 5 serrano chiles, depending on the amount of heat desired
 1 garlic clove, unpeeled
 2 cilantro sprigs
 Salt

1 Heat a comal or a medium saucepan over medium-low heat. When the pan is hot, place the tomatillos, chile(s), and garlic onto the pan and grill, turning them with tongs just once or twice on each side, until all of the ingredients have picked up some charred spots, about 20 minutes. As the tomatillos are ready, transfer them to a blender. As the chile(s) and garlic are ready, transfer them to a plate.

2 Stem the chile(s) and peel the garlic, then add them to the blender along with the cilantro and ½ teaspoon salt. Grind the ingredients, pulsing two or three times or more, until the salsa is the consistency you prefer, whether coarse, smooth, or somewhere in between. Taste for salt and add more if needed. If the salsa is too thick, add water, a couple of teaspoons at a time, to achieve a thinner consistency. You can instead use a *molcajete* (see page 197) to grind the salsa: start by adding the garlic and some salt, then the chile(s) and cilantro, and finally the tomatillos, grinding after the addition of each ingredient until it is the consistency you prefer.

3 Serve at once, or store in a glass jar in the refrigerator for up to 5 days.

Mexican Tomato Sauce
Caldillo de Jitomate

Makes about 3½ cups
 8 medium Roma tomatoes, quartered
 ½ medium white onion, halved
 1 garlic clove
 1 cup water
 Salt
 1 tablespoon canola oil
 4 cilantro sprigs

1 In a blender, combine the tomatoes, onion, garlic, water, and ½ teaspoon salt and blend until smooth. Strain through a fine-mesh sieve into a nonreactive medium bowl.

2 Heat a 12-inch skillet over medium heat. When the pan is hot, add the oil. When the oil is hot, add the strained sauce and stand back, as the sauce will splatter. Turn down the heat to medium-low, add the cilantro, and simmer until the sauce no longer tastes raw, 7 to 10 minutes. Taste for salt and add more if needed. If you like, remove the cilantro sprigs before using.

3 The sauce can be used right away, or it can be stored in an airtight container in the refrigerator for up to a few days.

Salt The recipes in this book were tested with an unrefined fine sea salt, using an intentionally light touch. In getting saltiness right in your dishes, add it incrementally: use just as much as the recipe calls for, let that absorb before tasting, and then continue to taste the dish until it makes it to the table. It's important to find a salt that you like and to get to know it—to learn how intense it is and how much to add to your liking. Not all salt is created equal: there's a wide gulf between the results you'll get from a good sea salt, say, and a supermarket table salt, which can be forceful in saltiness. Even among better salts, each behaves differently and has varying degrees of intensity. Find a good-quality pure sea salt and grind it yourself—an easy and rewarding task. A good second choice are the numerous types of kosher salt, such as Morton's, which is a light, coarse-grained variety that has a direct flavor and melts very rapidly in both hot and cold dishes.

Tortilla Chips These iconic Mexican snacks can, of course, be bought almost anywhere food is sold (look for those with the fewest ingredients listed on the package), but homemade chips taste better and are far more wholesome.

Tortilla Chips
Totopos

Use tortillas that are at least a few days old—they'll yield crispier chips.

Makes about 10 cups
 4 to 5 cups canola oil, for deep-frying
 16 stale 6-inch corn tortillas, each cut into six triangles
 Salt

1 Line a plate with paper towels. In a heavy medium saucepan, pour the oil to a depth of about 3 inches and heat over medium-high heat. To test if the oil is ready, drop in a small scrap of tortilla; if bubbles form around it instantly, the oil is ready. Add about 15 tortilla triangles to the hot oil and fry, turning the pieces frequently, until each piece is barely golden and crispy, 3½ to 4 minutes total. During the frying process, you will likely need to adjust the heat, raising and lowering it to avoid scorching or burning the triangles. Transfer the tortilla chips to the plate. Fry the remaining triangles in batches the same way, adding more oil to the pan as needed.

2 Sprinkle the tortilla chips with salt to taste and serve. Leftovers can be stored in an airtight container at room temperature for up to a few days.

Tostadas Crisply cooked whole corn tortillas, tostadas can be prepared in the oven on a sheet pan or oven rack or on the stove top in a hot skillet; they are better tasting and have superior texture to the store-bought variety. You must use stale tortillas.

   Oven Tostadas Preheat the oven on its lowest setting for 10 minutes. Arrange the tortillas in a single layer on a sheet pan or, even better, directly on the oven rack, where they will be heated more evenly. Bake the tortillas until golden and crisp, 15 to 20 minutes. Let cool completely before serving.

   Fried Tostadas Line a plate with paper towels. Heat a small skillet over medium heat. When the pan is hot, add canola oil to a depth of ½ inch. To test if the oil is ready, drop in a small scrap of tortilla; if bubbles form around it instantly, the oil is ready. Add a tortilla and fry until golden and crispy on the first side, about 1 minute. Flip the tortilla and fry the second side until golden and crispy, 1 minute. Transfer to the plate. Repeat with as many tortillas as desired, adding more oil to the pan as needed.

Vegetables are best purchased at farmers' markets, or at any market with quality produce.

   White Onion ② Called for in most of the savory recipes in this book, white onions have a fresher taste than cured yellow onions. The ones pictured here have their greens still attached, but generally they are sold without them. White onions are widely available in supermarkets; select specimens that are firm and heavy for their size. Stored at room temperature, they will keep for a somewhat shorter time than yellow onions.

   Nopal ⑥ Paddles of the nopal cactus, nopales are available in the produce section of Mexican grocery stores and sometimes at Whole Foods and other well-stocked supermarkets. They range in size from about 4 to 9 inches, with the smaller ones more tender. Select firm, bright-green paddles with no signs of bruising or deterioration. They are usually sold with their hairlike thorns already removed. Those with thorns intact stay fresh longer, however, so if you want to clean your own, grab the narrow end of the paddle with a folded kitchen towel and scrape off the thorns on both sides with a sharp knife. Nopales are best eaten right away but can be wrapped in plastic wrap and refrigerated in the crisper for a few days. Note that the recipes in this book call for fresh nopales. Jarred nopales are a tasty addition to scrambled eggs but won't yield the same results.

   Purslane ① An edible succulent that grows wild in summertime, purslane is often available at farmers' markets, specialty produce grocers, and Mexican stores, where it is known as *verdolagas*. Choose as you would lettuce, selecting the crispest and freshest-looking bunch, and store in a plastic bag in the refrigerator crisper for up to a couple of days. Rinse well before use to eliminate any sandy soil trapped among the leaves.

   Tomatillo ③ Resembling small green tomatoes with an inedible papery husk, tomatillos have a slightly sticky skin. They are widely available at

Mexican grocers and mainstream supermarkets. Look for fresh, bright lime-green specimens with no discoloration. Store as you would tomatoes, at room temperature, or in the crisper for about 1 week.

Chayote ⑤ About the size of a squat green pear, chayote has a mild squash-like flavor. The seeds are edible, but fibrous matter that runs down the center can be cut away and discarded. Chayotes are sometimes available in supermarkets; look for firm specimens with taut, glossy skin. Store in a plastic bag in the crisper for up to a week or so.

Zucchini Blossom ④ Widely available in farmers' markets, produce markets, and vegetable gardens during summer, the blossoms of the zucchini plant are delicious cooked in stews or simply sautéed with olive oil, garlic, salt, and pepper.

Choose the freshest-looking flowers and use the same day if possible, or wrap loosely in dampened paper towels, slip into a plastic bag, and store in the refrigerator crisper for up to a day or two.

Iceberg Lettuce (not shown) is used to garnish Mexican dishes because it holds up to the heat of a freshly-cooked dish without losing its crunch. Other varieties should not be substituted. Try to buy iceberg lettuce at a farmers' market if possible, for its appealingly sweet flavor and crispness.

Mezcal and Tequila, An Intoxicating Gift

The agave plant is as emblematic of Mexico as corn. When the Spanish conquistador Hernán Cortés first arrived, he wrote of its ubiquity and utility: the spiky succulent—not a cactus, as is often assumed—provided food and water, needle and thread, weapon and armor. These days, it's best known as the source of Mexico's most intoxicating gift to the world.

Mezcal refers to any distillate from the *maguey* plant, the Mexican word for agave. Tequila, a variation of mezcal, is made (by law) from at least 51 percent Weber blue agave, much as Champagne is one kind of wine made in one region of France. It is produced (again, by law) in only five Mexican states: Jalisco, parts of Michoacán, Guanajuato, Nayarit, and Tamaulipas. The mature Weber blue agave plant is stripped of its leaves to reveal its *piña* (pineapple), which is cooked until soft and sweet and crushed to extract the juice. The juice is then fermented and distilled.

As is the case with wine, the flavor and body of mezcal can be affected by any of the thirty-plus types of maguey used to make it, their terroir, and how it is prepared; even the native yeasts in the air that spur fermentation lend an influence. But unlike grapevines, which provide annual crops, agaves cannot be used until mature (usually between six and thirty years, depending on variety).

Mezcal is typically served with orange slices dusted with fine sea salt flavored with árbol chile powder; tequila is frequently served with Sangrita (page 190) or with lime and salt. Bear in mind that while tequila is usually 38 to 45 percent alcohol, mezcal is commonly 46 to 54 percent, so tread carefully. Try different brands until you find characteristics you enjoy most; every bottle comes marked with its place of production, the name of the producer, a lot number, and its grade of alcohol. As is the case with any spirit, imbibing a truly quality mezcal is a rewarding experience, whether you drink it as an accompaniment to a boldly seasoned dish like Cantina-Style Shrimp with Carrots, Chiles, Olives, and Potatoes (page 112), in a cocktail, or on its own. —*Nils Bernstein, food editor at* Wine Enthusiast *magazine*

WORLD FOOD

Editor and Author James Oseland
Creative Director Dave Weaver
Executive Editor Jenna Leigh Evans
World Food Test Kitchen Director Brenda Nieto
Kitchen Assistants Nora Bergen, Libia Brenda,
Esther Guzman, Jeffrey Lan
Researchers Taylor Cannon, Pablo Orube
Mexico City Advisors Nils Bernstein, Libia
Brenda, Margot Castañeda, Laura Cohen, Alfredo
Gavaldón, David Lida, Cristina Potters,
Nadia Santillanes

Bibliography

Bayless, Rick. *Authentic Mexican: Regional
      Cooking from the Heart of Mexico.*
      New York: William Morrow, 1987.
Bayless, Rick. *Mexico: One Plate at a Time.*
      New York: Scribner, 2000.
Kandell, Jonathan. *La Capital: The Biography of
      Mexico City.* New York: Random House, 1988.
Kennedy, Diana. *The Art of Mexican Cooking.*
      New York: Bantam Books, 1989.
Kennedy, Diana. *The Cuisines of Mexico.*
      New York: Harper & Row, 1972.
Lida, David. *First Stop in the New World:
      Mexico City, the Capital of the 21st Century.*
      New York: Riverhead Books, 2008.
Novo, Salvador. *Cocina mexicana: Historia
      gastronómica de la ciudad de México.*
      Mexico City: Porrua, 1967.
Quintana, Patricia. *The Taste of Mexico.*
      New York: Stewart, Tabori & Chang, 1986.
Rombauer, Irma S., Marion Rombauer Becker, and
      Ethan Becker. *Joy of Cooking.* New York:
      Scribner, 1997.

Acknowledgments

Many people helped in the making of
this book, the premiere volume of World
Food. In particular, I would like to express my
gratitude to Jill Goodman for her wisdom and
guidance; Doe Coover, my agent, for her
belief in World Food; and Hannah Rahill, my
publisher, for her insightful support. I would
also like to thank Mennlay Aggrey; Betsy
Andrews; Mario Aranda; Massimo Audiello;
Robin Brewer; Javier Cabral; Casa Jacaranda
cooking school (Alberto Estúa and Jorge
Fitz); Jesus Chairez; Mario Martínez Chávez;
Vivian Cohen and her family; Beatriz de la
Rosa; Naomi Duguid; Ernesto Silvio Escobar;
Verónica Sánchez Félix; Itzia Fernández;
Alam Méndez Florián; Alma Galindo and her
family; Nicholas Gilman; José de Jesús León
Hernández; Victoria Hernández and her
family; Amanda Hesser; Jim Johnston; Beth
Kracklauer; La Comida Chiva; La Salvación
Café; Maïna Le Marchand; Mónica Casanova;
Ricardo Regules García; Merrie Lawson; Erin
Lewis; Óscar Luviano; Josue Macias; Daniel
Manrique; Karla Marin; Rachel Markowitz;
Rita Marmor; David McAninch; Estella
Mejido; Gabriela Damián Miravete and her
family; Andrea Nguyen; Iliana Nieto; Martha
Ortiz; Gustavo Orube; Victoria Orube; Julie
Oseland; Alvany Padilla; Michael Parker;
Mónica Patiño; Sofia Perez; David Plotnikoff;
Francine Prose; Yesenia Ruiz; Harris Salat;
Rebecca Saletan; Alexis Scott; Margie
Schnibbe; Sharon Silva; Thor Stockman;
Dave Serwatka; Alex Suástegui; Maddy
Sweitzer-Lamme; Leah Tannehill; Sarah
Tannehill-Garza; the dedicated team at Ten
Speed Press; Tepito Arte Acá; Lesley Tellez;
John R. Thompson; Susan Traylor; Naomi
Uman; Verónica Velásquez; Vijayan Swami;
and Nick Zedd.

Index

Library of Congress Cataloging-in-Publication Data
  Names: Oseland, James, author.
  Title: Mexico city : Heritage Recipes for Classic Home Cooking /
    James Oseland.
  Description: First edition. | New York : Ten Speed Press, 2020. |
    Includes bibliographical references and index.
  Identifiers: LCCN 2019053522 | ISBN 9780399579851 (hardcover) |
    ISBN 9780399579868 (epub)
  Subjects: LCSH: Cooking, Mexican. | LCGFT: Cookbooks.
  Classification: LCC TX716.M4 O84 2020 | DDC 641.5972—dc23
    LC record available at https://lccn.loc.gov/2019053522

Hardcover ISBN: 978-0-399-57985-1
eBook ISBN: 978-0-399-57986-8

Printed in China

Photos on pages 17, 46, and 65 are owned by Fototeca Nacional INAH.

Design by David Weaver
Food and prop styling by James Oseland
Map by Mike Hall

10 9 8 7 6 5 4 3 2 1

First Edition